Changes in communal provision for adult social care 1991–2001

✓ Available in alternative formats

This publication can be provided in alternative formats, such as large print, Braille, audiotape and on disk. Please contact: Communications Department, Joseph Rowntree Foundation, The Homestead, 40 Water End, York YO30 6WP.
Tel: 01904 615905. Email: info@jrf.org.uk

Changes in communal provision for adult social care 1991–2001

Laura Banks, Philip Haynes, Susan Balloch and Michael Hill

JOSEPH ROWNTREE FOUNDATION

The **Joseph Rowntree Foundation** has supported this project as part of its programme of research and innovative development projects, which it hopes will be of value to policy makers, practitioners and service users. The facts presented and views expressed in this report are, however, those of the authors and not necessarily those of the Foundation.

Joseph Rowntree Foundation
The Homestead
40 Water End
York YO30 6WP
Website: www.jrf.org.uk

© University of Brighton 2006

First published 2006 by the Joseph Rowntree Foundation

All rights reserved. Reproduction of this report by photocopying or electronic means for non-commercial purposes is permitted. Otherwise, no part of this report may be reproduced, adapted, stored in a retrieval system or transmitted by any means, electronic, mechanical, photocopying, or otherwise without the prior written permission of the Joseph Rowntree Foundation.

ISBN-13: 978 185935 485 8
ISBN-10: 1 85935 485 8

A pdf version of this publication is available from the JRF website (www.jrf.org.uk).

A CIP catalogue record for this report is available from the British Library.

Cover design by Adkins Design

Prepared and printed by:
York Publishing Services Ltd
64 Hallfield Road
Layerthorpe
York YO31 7ZQ
Tel: 01904 430033;   Fax: 01904 430868;   Website: www.yps-publishing.co.uk

Further copies of this report, or any other JRF publication, can be obtained either from the JRF website (www.jrf.org.uk/bookshop/) or from our distributor, York Publishing Services Ltd, at the above address.

Contents

Acknowledgements	vii
Executive summary	viii
1 Introduction	1
Background	2
Methods	3
2 Key changes 1991–2001	5
Key findings	5
Changes by type of care home	6
Regional changes in homes and residents	7
Changes in age distribution	11
Changes in the care home population in relation to the total population size	13
Conclusion	17
3 Variations between local authority areas	18
Key findings	18
Supported residents in England and Wales	19
Supported residents in Scotland	23
Local government performance	25
Political control and change in urban areas	26
Variations by area classification	27
Demography	33
Poverty and health indicators	38
Property prices	43
Conclusion	46
4 Gender and marital status	47
Key findings	47
Gender and residential care by age groups	48
Marital status and residential care by age groups	50
The relationship between marital status, gender and age	51
Conclusion	53
5 Ethnicity	54
Key findings	54
Ethnicity and residential care by age groups	55
Ethnicity and residential care by area	56
Ethnicity and informal care	59
Conclusion	61

6	**Relationship between residential care and other types of care**	62
	Key findings	62
	Home care services	62
	Unpaid care	64
	Conclusion	67
7	**Conclusions**	68
	The type of homes in decline	69
	Country and regional variations	70
	Scotland	70
	Local authority area variations	71
	Possible concerns for local communities in Inner London	72
	Older people and ethnic minorities	73
	Women and care homes	73
	Age groups	74
	Coastal and rural areas	74
	Poverty and residential care	75
	Working with the market to meet local social needs	75

Notes	77
References	82
Appendix 1: Northern Ireland	84
Appendix 2: Geographical areas 1991/2001	90
Appendix 3: Census information	95

Acknowledgements

Our thanks to the organisations that have supplied data for this research. These include the Office of National Statistics, The Department of Health, The Land Registry for England and Wales, The National Assembly for Wales, The Local Government Data Unit for Wales, The Scottish Executive and Scottish Statistics. We are also grateful for the support of the ESRC/JISC academic programme for the 1991 and 2001 Censuses, in particular the Census Dissemination Unit at the University of Manchester and the Cathie Marsh Centre for Census and Survey Research at the University of Manchester, which supports the Samples of Anonymised Records (SARs).

Our thanks also for advice and expertise received from: Enid Levin, Emily Grundy, John Knight, Valerie Williamson, Martin Knapp, Kate Davidson, Helen Charnley, Anne Harrop, Janice Robinson, Paul Spicker, Madhavi Bajekal, Geoff Peasah and all those who attended the University of Brighton seminar on 20 May 2005.

Executive summary

This report explores changes in patterns of residential and nursing care in the UK between 1991 and 2001, using census data from both years. General trends in these services were examined with additional consideration of the changing age, gender and ethnic compositions of care home populations in relation to wider demographic change. The research was carried out by Laura Banks, Philip Haynes, Susan Balloch and Michael Hill of the Health and Social Policy Research Centre, University of Brighton.

Key overall findings set out in *Chapter 2* include the following.

- There had been a decline in nursing and residential care homes in Great Britain of −11 per cent, between 1991 and 2001. However, as shown in Figure 1, overall, there was a slight increase in care homes in the independent sector. This was not, however, evident in Wales, which saw a decline in both sectors.

- Scotland was the only country in Great Britain where there was an increase in the total number (local authority and independent sector combined) of care homes (+11 per cent). One reason for this appears to have been the closing of large institutions, which happened later than in England and Wales.

- There was a slight increase in the independent sector in Northern Ireland but local authority data on homes and residents was not comparable between 1991 and 2001. This is explored in Appendix 1 of the report.

Chapter 3 explores variations between local authority areas in Great Britain showing the following.

- Decline in residential and nursing care had greater impact in urban areas. Older people in urban areas were less likely to be living in care homes. Urban local authorities were, however, more likely than rural/mixed areas to support residents living in care homes in other local authority areas.

- Decline in residential and nursing care tended to be greater in more deprived areas with poorer levels of health. This raises concerns that care homes are not necessarily located where they are most socially needed.

Executive summary

- Many Inner London boroughs were identified as the greatest 'exporters' (i.e. having larger numbers of supported care home residents than total care home residents living in the local authority area) in 2001. The lack of local care provision may be a particular concern in terms of the impact this may have on poorer Londoners and those from ethnic minorities who may be reluctant to move away from their local community.

- Areas with the lowest ratios of supported residents to total residents were in coastal areas of the South West and South East of England. Therefore it seems likely that these areas also have the large numbers of residents exported from other areas.

Chapter 4 sets out findings in relation to gender and marital status, and shows that women were over-represented in care homes in both 1991 and 2001, even allowing for the trend for women to outlive men.

Chapter 5 explores ethnicity in relation to care home residents and shows that, when controlling for age, in both 1991 and 2001 people from ethnic minorities were less likely to be living in care homes than those from the white majority population. The decline in care homes in London had a greater proportional impact on people from ethnic minorities than white people in the area.

Chapter 6 considers the relationship between residential and other types of care showing that there was no uniform association between local authorities experiencing a greater decline in residential/nursing care provision and a growth in home care services.

Chapter 7 sets out the conclusions from the authors' analysis of data from the 1991 and 2001 Censuses of patterns of residential and nursing care in the UK.

1 Introduction

The purpose of this research is to examine changes in patterns of residential and nursing care in the UK between 1991 and 2001 following the introduction of the 1990 NHS and Community Care Act. The research uses the detailed data available on the number of homes and residents as provided in the Censuses taken in those two years. The main analysis is for Great Britain, but there is an analysis in Appendix 1 on Northern Ireland. The research examined the general trends in these services, with additional consideration of the changing age, gender, ethnic and urban–rural profile of residential care. Specific aims included to:

- measure changes in the residential care population and the *number and type of establishments* 1991–2001, and to assess geographical variations in these changes

- explore changes in care home provision in different types of geographical area

- measure whether there were any significant changes in the gender populations of residential care and any associated geographical complexities

- measure whether older people from ethnic minorities have the same levels of local access to residential care as other population groups

- examine changes between 1991 and 2001, and consider associated geographical complexities

- explore associations between changes in the pattern of residential care provision and changes in patterns of other provision, for example supported home care.

In addition to census data, further information on social care services and their financing was used from the Department of Health, Welsh Assembly Office (previously the Welsh Office) and the Scottish Executive. Some supporting documentary analysis was also undertaken using government documents, circulars and inspection reports prepared by the Joint Reviews of Social Services. Joint Review inspection reports of local authority social care performance were taken from the Joint Review website at http://www.joint-reviews.gov.uk/.

Changes in communal provision for adult social care 1991–2001

Background

In the 1980s there was an exponential increase in residential care for adults with long-term limiting illnesses. National sources indicated that, between 1979 and 1989, the public-funded residential care population increased in England and Wales from expenditure of several million pounds to over £1 billion in expenditure (Department of Health, 1989). Much of this was linked initially to changes in social security regulations in the early 1980s, as this opened up relatively easy access to a growing market in private care when compared with the local authority procedures of means testing and assessment for local authority provision. The bulk of this growth in residential provision was for older people, but significant numbers of people with mental health problems also moved from state institutions, such as hospitals and local authority homes, to private and charitable run homes. Transition rates to care institutions were much higher for older people in 1981–91 than in 1971–81 (Grundy and Glaser, 1997). These changes were well documented (Audit Commission, 1986) and the Audit Commission coined the phrase 'the perverse incentive', given the lack of comparable growth in services for home care.

Following the major review of social care established by the Conservative Government in the late 1980s (Griffiths, 1989), the NHS and Community Care Act 1990 established an important change in policy whereby the allocation of provision for poorer older people was once again under the control of local authorities, with less direct access being facilitated by social security payments. In time, this policy resulted in a consolidation of residential bed provision and a gradual focus on the development of better community care alternatives, although with a continuing concern that all social care was difficult to access and fund. The result was that many families and partners continued to provide informal care that was often unsupported by the State (Bulmer, 1987).

In 1998 the New Labour policy on social care was introduced in Modernising Social Services, a policy that promised a more systematic development of quality and better alternatives to residential provision. Concerns remained about the levels of funding available and whether local developments could keep pace with rising demand. Previous inspections of individual local authorities carried out by the Audit Commission and Social Services Inspectorate for the Department of Health suggested serious geographical inequities in the current social care market.

Newspaper and television reports began to focus on the decline of both local authority and private residential care, with the suggestion that price fixing by local government, coupled with rising property prices, encouraged private owners to sell

Introduction

up. Consolidation of the residential sector resulted in some older people having to be moved from one home to another, sometimes against their will. The tabloid press gave prominence to very old residents forced to move out of residential provision to be located at alternative homes. Nevertheless, local authorities that had tried to retain their own stock of public residential provision were often criticised by the Department of Health and Audit Commission joint review process and they increasingly looked to move their resources into the purchase of home care and short-term residential respite care. The overall success of this policy change was far from clear. In 2003 the National Audit Office began to raise concerns about the decline of care home beds because of the likely effect this was having on delaying discharges from hospital (National Audit Office, 2003, Executive Summary, para. 19). It was particularly concerned about the effect this was having in London and the South East.

Publication of the 2001 Census presented an opportunity to analyse the scale of residential provision in Great Britain, to examine changes in relation to 1991 and geographical variations such as differences between urban and rural, and rich and poor areas, and what had happened in those parts of the country traditionally seen as retirement areas and previously identified as having large numbers of residential establishments. The large scale of the census database offered an opportunity to better understand the complexities of these questions when compared to standard government health and social care statistics, and private consultancy based studies for the market. One consultancy study offering an annual return from the sector on declining residential beds estimates a decrease of 13,100 beds in 2001.[1] Although the Department of Health also seeks to monitor these changes independently of the private sector there are some concerns over the reliability of local government returns to the Department of Health. As such, the Census offered an opportunity to cross-triangulate information, given the much more detailed data submitted by individuals and those in charge of communal establishments.

Methods

The main method of this research is the analysis of already existing secondary government data. This data varies in its format and reliability, and a full technical account of the strengths and limitations of the data is given in Appendix 3.

Changes in communal provision for adult social care 1991–2001

Geographical analysis

Great Britain experienced a changing socio-political geography between 1991 and 2001. Social care service administration boundaries changed in many parts of the country following the local government reorganisation of 1995–96. In addition, at a higher geographical coverage, the 2001 Census provided outputs in the new regional government areas for England. In both cases, the method for making output areas comparable was to map back from the 2001 Census definitions.

This resulted in the same geographical areas, rather than the same named authorities, being compared. For example, East Sussex in 2001 is compared with the statistics from the identical geographical sub-area of East Sussex in 1991 (excluding the geography now covered by the new unitary authority of Brighton and Hove, which was previously part of East Sussex).[2]

Similarly, 2001 English regions were replicated with 1991 data, using previous county tables. This approach was possible because of the complex layered geographical coverage offered by the Censuses and the ability to deconstruct the statistics of larger areas into smaller components. The result is that the same scope of geographical locations and boundaries are compared.[3] There is some difference in the regions used by the SAR (Sample of Anonymised Records) for 1991 and 2001. However, this does not affect most of the regional comparisons between 1991 and 2001 because the calculations are based on 2001 regional geographies using full census data. In the few places where regional changes are modelled using SAR data, and this includes unstable regional definitions, this problem is indicated in the text.

Statistical analysis

This report uses a variety of statistical methods, including tables, figures and maps. Scatterplots are also used on a number of occasions. These examine the relationship between two variables. It should be noted that R Squared Linear is computed in these plots, and gives a line of how one variable would best predict the other. But, in the text, a different but related calculation r is given. This is the correlation coefficient that examines the direction and strength of association between the two variables. For guidance, a value of $r = 1$ indicates a perfect association, a value of 0.5 a moderate association.

Note: Crown copyright material is reproduced with the permission of the Controller of HMSO and the Queen's Printer for Scotland.

2 Key changes 1991–2001

This chapter presents the changes in residential and nursing care by country and region of Britain. These include the numbers of homes and residents in such homes, as well as changes in age distribution within care homes and in relation to changes in the wider population.

Key findings

Key changes 1991–2001 identified in this chapter include the following.

1 *Changes that are universal to Britain:*
   - a decline in local authority care home provision
   - variation in the independent sector, with an overall increase in residential care and a decline in nursing care
   - a decline in the number of people aged 75–84 in care homes despite an increase in the total population
   - an increase in the number of people aged 85 and over living in care homes, but below the rate of increase in the wider population
   - a decline in the number of people aged 16–74 living in care homes, which was in line with the decline in the number of people in this age group in the general population
   - an increase in the average age of someone living in a care home because of the growth in the number of people aged 90 and over and a decline in the number of people under 30
   - a narrowing in the differences between regions in terms of the proportion of people living in care homes.

2 *Changes specific to some countries or regions:*
   - the North West and Wales were the two regions to have experienced the greatest proportionate decline in total homes and residents
   - Scotland was the only region to have seen an overall increase in the number of homes and residents
   - Scotland was the only region to have seen an increase in the proportion of people aged 75 and over living in care homes
   - in both years, London was the region with the lowest proportion of people living in care homes (this was true for all age groups except for the under 75s in 1991).

Changes in communal provision for adult social care 1991–2001

Changes by type of care home

As outlined in Appendix 3, the term 'care homes' used in this report includes the census categories:

- local authority homes (excluding children's homes)

- nursing homes (non-NHS) private and independent sector

- residential homes (non-NHS/local authority/health authority) private and independent sector.

In Figure 1, changes in the number of the three types of homes within the countries of Great Britain are presented for comparison. They indicate that, overall, the trend in the independent sector has been an increase in residential care but a decline in the number of nursing homes. Different trends were, however, apparent in Scotland and Wales. In Scotland there was an increase in nursing homes (as well as independent residential care homes). In Wales there was a decline in independent residential homes and a particularly large decline in nursing homes. All countries saw a decline in local authority care homes, although this was much greater in England and least dramatic in Scotland.[1]

Figure 1 Percentage change in local authority and independent sector residential and nursing homes by country, 1991–2001

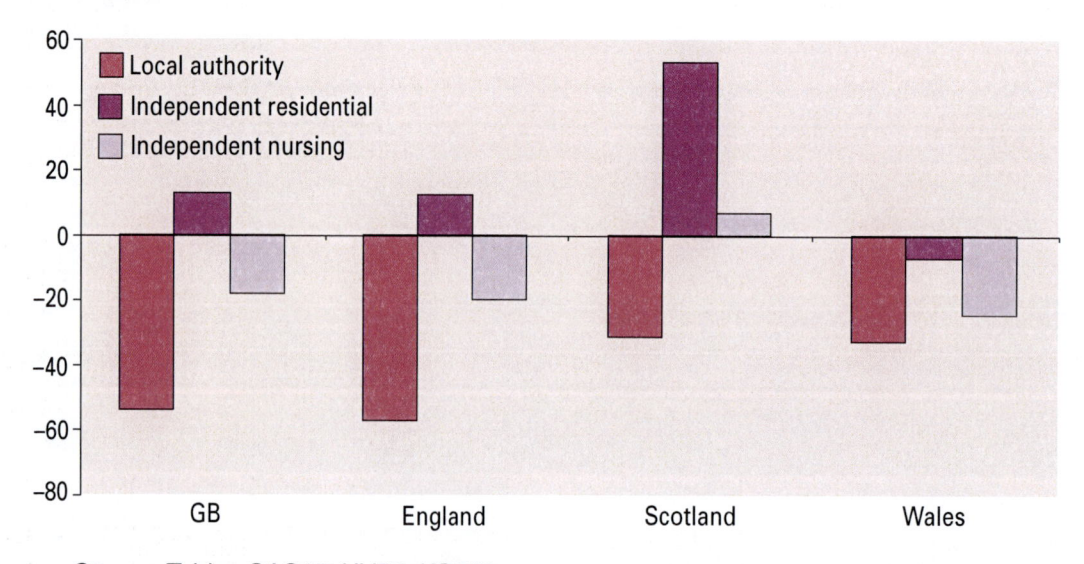

Sources: Census Tables SAS03, UV70, KS023.

Key changes 1991–2001

Although these key changes by country have been separated into residential and nursing care, subsequent analysis at regional level combines these two types of establishment because of a concern about the lack of definition of dual-registered homes in the census data used.[2]

Regional changes in homes and residents

This section presents the changes in homes and residents by Government Office region and sector.

Overall changes

When the changes in the two sectors are combined, as in Table 1, it shows that there was an overall decline in homes and residents, but this is offset by an increase in Scotland of 137 homes and 6,028 residents (and also a slight increase of residents in the East of England).

Table 1 Total homes and residents 1991–2001 by English region and country of Great Britain

Region	Homes 1991	Homes 2001	Change homes No.	Change homes %	Residents 1991	Residents 2001	Change residents No.	Change residents %
North East	886	914	28	3.2	19,572	18,261	−1,311	−6.7
North West	3,183	2,526	−657	−20.6	61,140	46,809	−14,331	−23.4
Yorks and Humber	2,003	1,754	−249	−12.4	40,149	34,247	−5,902	−14.7
East Midlands	1,639	1,590	−49	−3.0	30,839	28,475	−2,364	−7.7
West Midlands	1,843	1,738	−105	−5.7	34,659	31,244	−3,415	−9.9
East	1,702	1,695	−7	−0.4	31,615	32,433	818	+2.6
London	1,627	1,456	−171	−10.5	31,250	25,618	−5,632	−18.0
South East	4,049	3,460	−589	−14.5	69,390	60,316	−9,074	−13.1
South West	3,300	2,771	−529	−16.0	53,093	44,947	−8,146	−15.3
England	20,232	17,904	−2,328	−11.5	371,707	322,350	−49,357	−13.3
Scotland	1,296	1,433	137	+10.6	28,171	34,199	6,028	+21.4
Wales	1,280	1,049	−231	−18.0	23,351	18,539	−4,812	−20.6
Great Britain	22,808	20,386	−2,422	−10.6	423,229	375,088	−48,141	−11.4

Sources: Census Tables SAS03, UV70, KS023.
Note: the Office of National Statistics (ONS) has advised that there was an undercount in 2001 care home resident statistics.

Changes in communal provision for adult social care 1991–2001

There is an interesting variation in changes in the English regions, with the North West, London, the South West and South East having declined the most. Table 1 shows the biggest impact to have been in the North West (−657 homes), South East (−589 homes) and South West (−529 homes), because these areas had a comparatively large number of homes and residents in 1991. In this context the decline in Wales (−231 homes) looks less substantial. This proportionately greater decline experienced in regions with a larger number of homes and residents in 1991 had an equalisation effect, i.e. in 2001 the difference between the regions was reduced. This is demonstrated in a reduction in the standard deviation for both homes (from 947 to 730) and residents (from 15,183 to 11,962).

Our research has also related changes in the number of care home residents to wider demographic change. These findings are discussed later in this chapter.

Changes in local authority owned care homes

Table 2 shows the decline in the number of local authority adult care homes and residents to have been relatively uniform across the whole of Great Britain. All regions saw a decline in homes ranging from −31 per cent in Scotland to −67 per cent in the South West, and a decline in residents ranging from the lowest, also in Scotland, of −38 per cent to the highest of −76 per cent in London.[3]

Table 2 Local authority homes and residents 1991–2001 by region/country of Great Britain

Region	Homes 1991	Homes 2001	Change homes No.	Change homes %	Residents 1991	Residents 2001	Change residents No.	Change residents %
North East	286	164	−122	−42.7	6,697	2,544	−4,153	−62.0
North West	708	316	−392	−55.4	15,290	5,038	−10,252	−67.1
Yorks and Humber	542	240	−302	−55.7	12,255	4,492	−7,763	−63.3
East Midlands	369	174	−195	−52.8	7,989	3,630	−4,359	−54.6
West Midlands	458	216	−242	−52.8	10,294	4,421	−5,873	−57.1
East	431	191	−240	−55.7	9,788	3,933	−5795	−59.2
London	572	201	−371	−64.9	12,863	3,122	−9,741	−75.7
South East	662	278	−384	−58.0	13,000	5,434	−7,566	−58.2
South West	529	173	−356	−67.3	9,731	2,846	−6,885	−70.8
England	4,557	1,953	−2,604	−57.1	97,907	35,520	−62,387	−63.7
Scotland	401	275	−126	−31.4	9,061	5,579	−3,482	−38.4
Wales	292	196	−96	−32.9	6,566	3,531	−3,035	−46.2
Great Britain	5,250	2,424	−2,826	−53.8	113,534	44,630	−68,904	−60.7

Sources: Census Tables SAS03, UV70, KS023.
Note: ONS has advised that there was an undercount in 2001 care home resident statistics.

Key changes 1991–2001

Changes in independent sector owned care homes

The changes in the independent sector (including both residential and nursing care) were much more varied than those evident in the local authority sector. Table 3 shows that, while the South East, South West, Wales and North West experienced a decline in the number of independent sector homes and residents, different rates of increase were apparent in other regions of the UK, with by far the largest increase evident in Scotland. This had the total effect of showing a small increase in the number of homes and residents for Britain as a whole.

Table 3 Independent sector homes and residents 1991–2001 by region/country of Great Britain

Region	Homes 1991	Homes 2001	Change homes No.	Change homes %	Residents 1991	Residents 2001	Change residents No.	Change residents %
North East	600	750	150	+25.0	12,875	15,717	2,842	+22.1
North West	2,475	2,210	−265	−10.7	45,850	41,771	−4,079	−8.9
Yorks and Humber	1,461	1,514	53	+3.6	27,894	29,755	1,861	+6.7
East Midlands	1,270	1,416	146	+11.5	22,850	24,845	1,995	+8.7
West Midlands	1,385	1,522	137	+10.0	24,365	26,823	2,458	+10.1
East	1,271	1,504	233	+18.3	21,827	28,440	6,613	+30.3
London	1,055	1,255	200	+19.0	18,387	22,496	4,109	+22.3
South East	3,387	3,182	−205	−6.1	56,390	54,882	−1,508	−2.7
South West	2,771	2,598	−173	−6.2	43,362	42,101	−1,261	−2.9
England	15,675	15,951	286	+1.8	273,800	286,830	13,030	+4.8
Scotland	895	1,158	263	+29.4	19,110	28,620	9,510	+49.8
Wales	988	853	−135	−13.7	16,785	15,008	−1,777	−10.6
Great Britain	17,558	17,962	404	+2.3	309,695	330,458	20,763	+6.7

Sources: Census Tables SAS03, UV70, KS023.
Note: ONS has advised that there was an undercount in 2001 care home resident statistics.

The relationship between changes in the local authority and independent sectors

One question that might arise from looking at the changes in numbers of care homes in the two sectors is whether there is any relationship between them. For example, is it the case that the private sector was more likely to have expanded in regions where there was a greater decline in local authority care, in order to compensate for this loss? Figure 2 indicates that this did not occur because, where there was a smaller decline in the number of local authority care homes, there tends to be a smaller decline in independent sector care homes. If investigated using a Pearson correlation coefficient this was found to be statistically significant ($r = 0.635$, $n = 10$,

Changes in communal provision for adult social care 1991–2001

$p = 0.049$). However, it did not include Wales. If Wales is included (see Figure 3) the correlation is not found to be significantly significant ($r = 0.222$, $n = 11$, $p = 0.512$). The situation in Wales was unusual in that, in comparison with the other regions of Great Britain, it experienced a small decline in local authority care alongside a relatively large decline in the independent sector. This different trend evident in Wales is investigated later in the report.

Figure 2 Scatterplot showing the relationship between the proportionate change 1991–2001 in local authority and independent sector care homes (by region, excluding Wales)

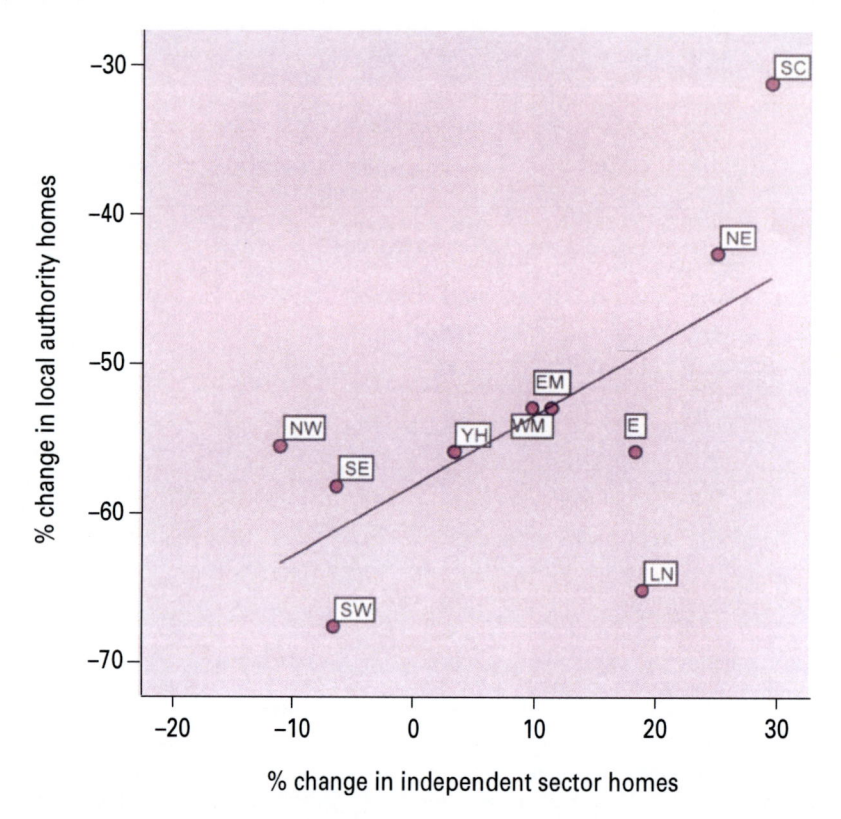

Sources: Census Tables SAS03, UV70, KS023.
Note: R Squared Linear = 0.403.

Key changes 1991–2001

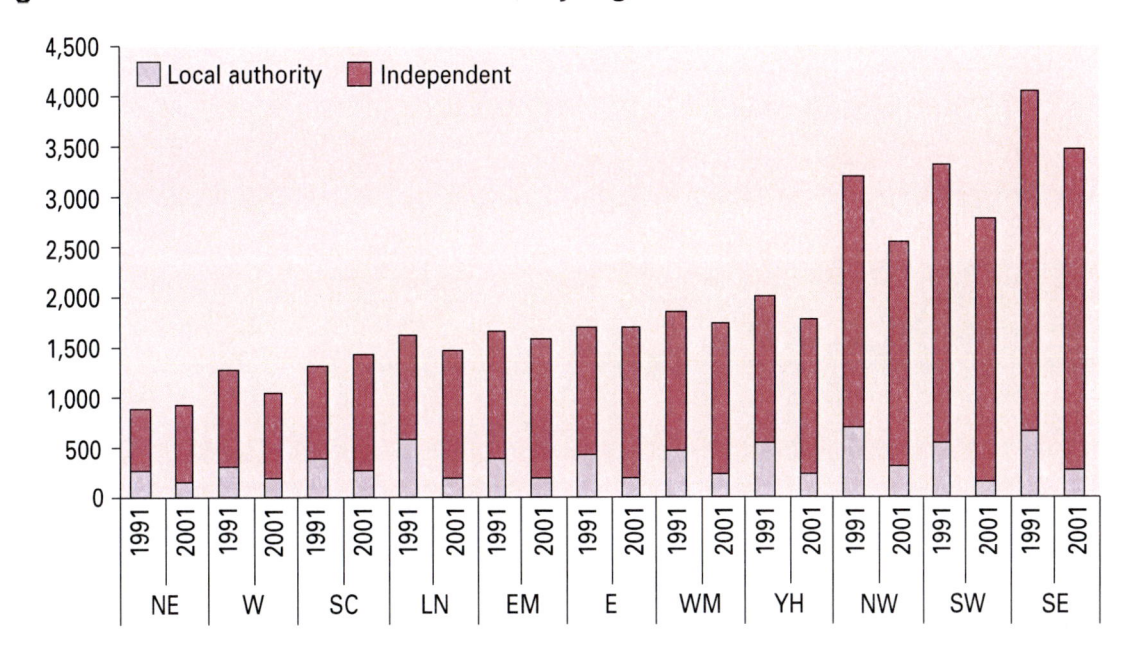

Figure 3 Number of homes 1991–2001 by region and sector

Sources: Census Tables SAS03, UV70, KS023.

Changes in age distribution

Changes in care homes

Of the three age groups presented in Table 4, the oldest (85 and over) was the only one to have increased overall. The table again highlights the differences in changes between the three countries, in particular showing increases in the number of residents in all age groups in Scotland, while in Wales the numbers in all three groups declined.

Table 4 Percentage changes in the number of persons living in care homes 1991–2001 by age group and country

	% change 16–74	% change 75–84	% change 85+
England	−16.1	−32.7	+6.6
Scotland	+26.8	+6.4	+36.7
Wales	−31.1	−44.6	−3.8
Great Britain	−14.3	−30.9	+8.1

Sources: Census Tables LBS04, ST126, ST232.

Changes in communal provision for adult social care 1991–2001

A comparison of the age distribution of the care home populations in 1991 and 2001 shows a similar trend emerging in England, Scotland and Wales. As shown in Table 5, the 85 and over age group as a proportion of the care home population increased in all countries (making up nearly half of the entire care home population in 2001). This occurs because this group increased the most numerically or, as in the case of Wales, declined the least. Despite an overall decline in the number of people aged under 75 (see Table 4), there was only a small decrease in the proportion of the care home population that was aged under 75, and, in Wales, there was actually a percentage increase (this is because the percentage decline in people in the 75–84 cohort was greater than the decline in the under 75 group).

Figure 4 gives a more detailed percentage breakdown (from SAR data) by age groups comprising the care home population of 1991 and 2001. Due to a smaller decline in the younger section of the care home population, there was a larger proportion of people aged under 65 living in care homes in 2001 (14.3 per cent) than in 1991 (11.8 per cent). The figure shows that all groups under 65 increased (as a total of the total care home population) except for the youngest group (16–29) and that, conversely, there was a proportionate decline in all age groups aged 65 and over, except for the oldest group (90+). This (i.e. the large increase in the oldest group and decline of the youngest) has resulted in an increase in the mean average age from 64 to 78 (it should be noted that these figures are skewed downwards due to the grouping of those aged 95+). The following section compares changes in the older care home resident population with general demographic change by region.

Table 5 Percentage of care home population by age group and country 1991–2001

	1991 % 16–74	1991 % 75–84	1991 % 85+	1991 % total	2001 % 16–74	2001 % 75–84	2001 % 85+	2001 % total
England	24.4	36.5	39.1	100	23.6	28.4	48.0	100
Scotland	23.0	36.3	40.7	100	22.3	31.8	45.9	100
Wales	15.1	44.5	40.4	100	19.9	31.1	49.0	100
Great Britain	23.8	37.0	39.2	100	23.3	28.8	47.9	100

Sources: Census Tables LBS04, ST126, ST232.

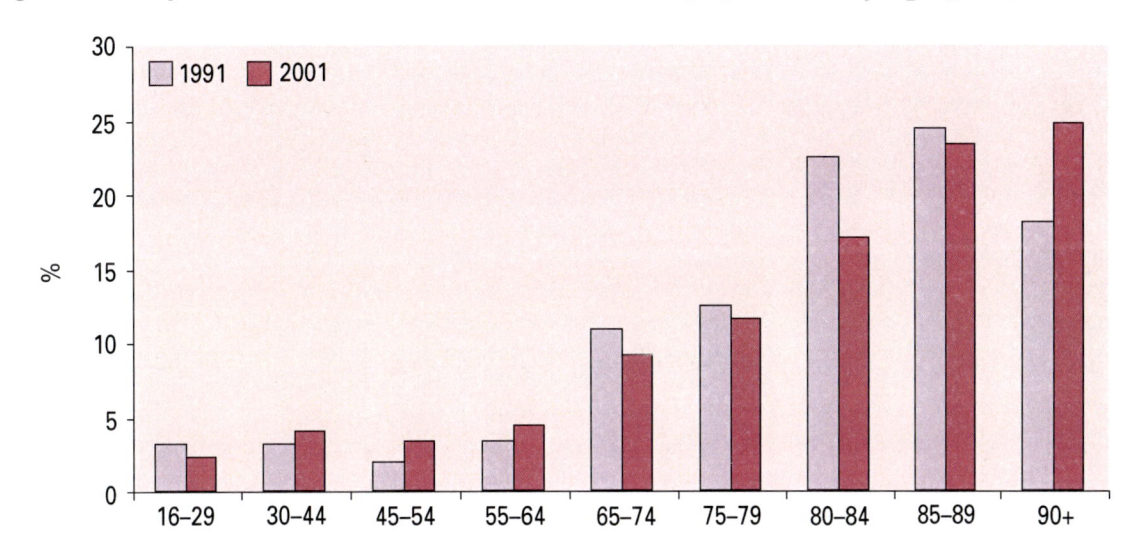

Figure 4 Proportion of the 1991–2001 care home population by age group

[Bar chart showing percentages by age group (16–29, 30–44, 45–54, 55–64, 65–74, 75–79, 80–84, 85–89, 90+) comparing 1991 and 2001.]

Source: Sample of Anonymised Records 1991–2001.

Changes in the care home population in relation to the total population size

In order to secure a better understanding of the substantive significance of changes in care home populations, it is necessary to view these in the context of wider demographic change. In particular, as a large majority of residents in care homes are over 75, it is important to identify changes by geographical area in the number of people who were in this age group at the time of the census counts.

Figures 5 and 6 illustrate the relationship between the changes in the total aged 75+ population and the number of people aged 75 and over living in care homes. Figure 5 highlights the increase in this age group in all regions except for London, where there was a marginal decline. Hence there is no association between a region having a falling care home population over time and a falling population of older people – because this is only true for London.

Figure 6 shows that, in regional areas where there are more people aged 75 and over in the general population, there also tended to be, as one would expect, a greater number of people in this age group living in care homes. The two scatterplots also allow comparison of changes in the relationships between regions over the ten-year period. For example, London continues to have a low level of residents aged 75 and over in care homes, in ratio to its population (London boroughs tend to have comparatively high numbers of local authority supported residents in other areas, as is discussed in Chapter 3), while Scotland has moved above the line and demonstrates its increased ratio of residents to population.

Changes in communal provision for adult social care 1991–2001

Figure 5 Residents aged 75+ in care homes, by the total population aged 75+ living in the region

Legend: 1991 residents aged 75+ ■ 2001 residents aged 75+ ■ 1991 total population aged 75+ — 2001 total population aged 75+

Sources: Census Tables LBS04, ST126, ST232, SAS02, KS02.
Notes: ONS has advised that there was an undercount in 2001 care home resident statistics.
Left axis is care home population, right axis is total population.

Figure 6a Scatterplot showing the relationship between the 75+ care home population and the 75+ total population by region, 1991

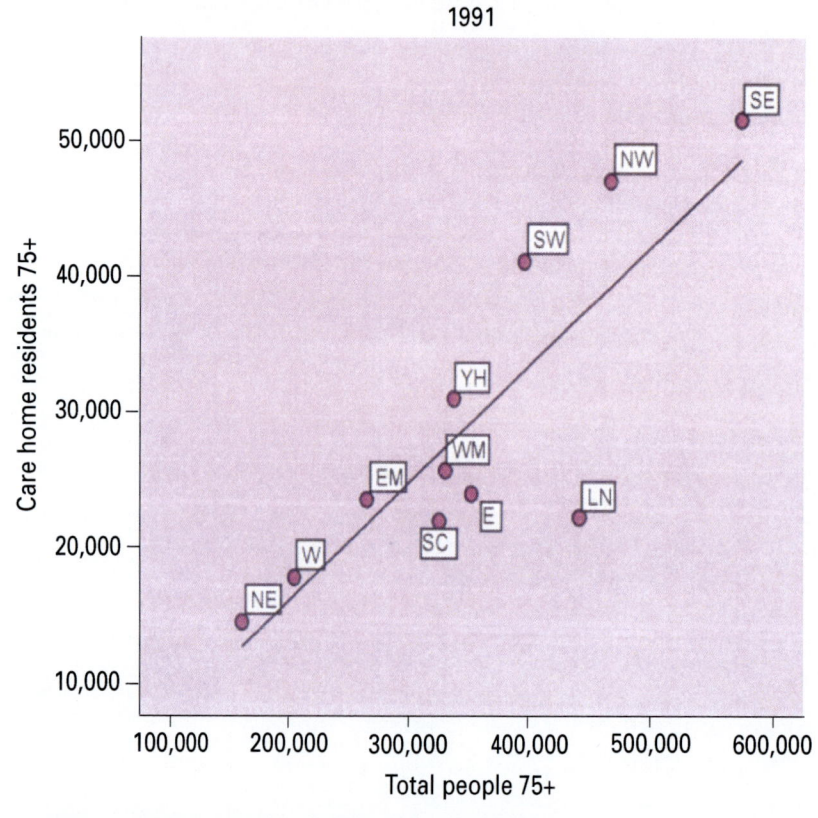

Sources: Census Tables LBS04, ST126, ST232, SAS02, KS02.
Notes: ONS has advised that there was an undercount in 2001 care home resident statistics.
R Squared Linear = 0.711.

Key changes 1991–2001

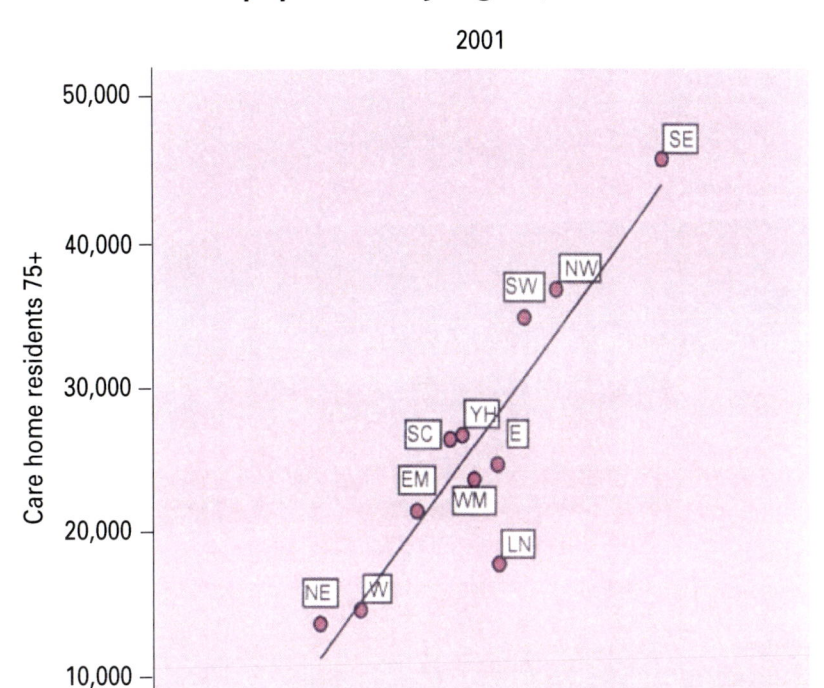

Figure 6b Scatterplot showing the relationship between the 75+ care home population and the 75+ total population by region, 2001

Sources: Census Tables LBS04, ST126, ST232, SAS02, KS02.
Notes: ONS has advised that there was an undercount in 2001 care home resident statistics.
R Squared Linear = 0.817.

As highlighted in Figure 7, a slightly different trend is evident for the 85+ population, with most regions having experienced an increase in numbers aged 85 and over, both in the total and in the care home population. Nevertheless, several (London, North West, South East and Wales) still saw a decline in the number of care home residents in this age group, and (except for Scotland where the aged 85 and over population had increased more rapidly in care homes than in the community) where there was an increase, this was much lower than the rate of change in the wider population. Thus, as is shown in Table 6, the proportion of people aged 85 and over living in residential care fell between 1991 and 2001 in all regions except Scotland. This is also true for the 75–84 age group. However, as the rate of decline in the number of people aged 16–74 in care homes was similar to the total population trend, the proportion of under 75's in care homes remained about the same in 2001.

Changes in communal provision for adult social care 1991–2001

Figure 7 Residents aged 85 or over in care homes by the total population aged 85 or over living in the region

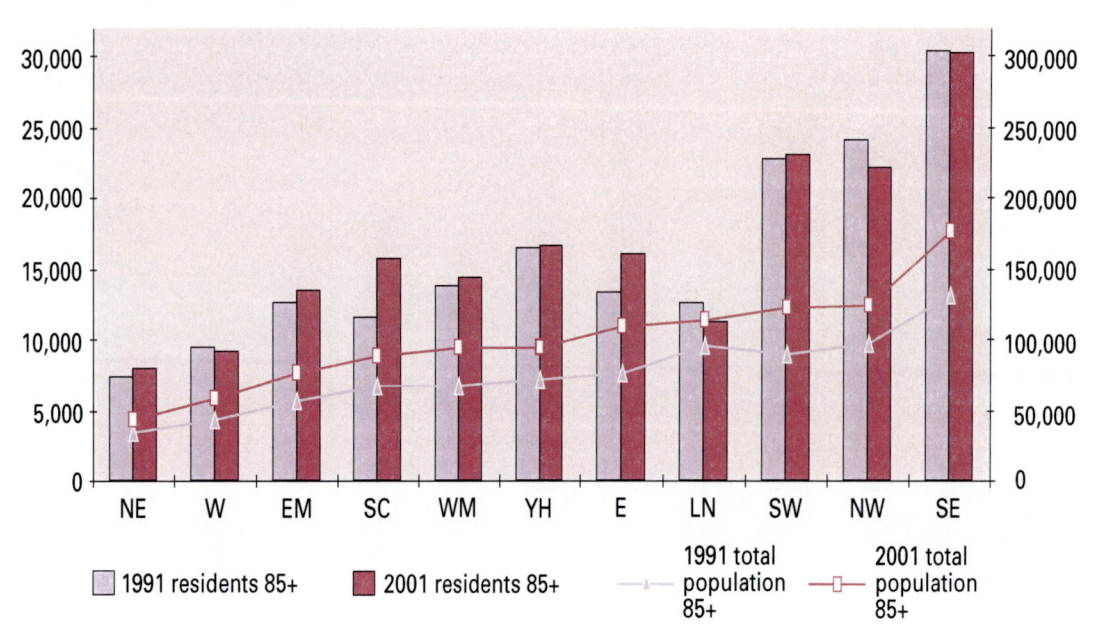

Sources: Census Tables LBS04, ST126, ST232, SAS02, KS02.
Notes: ONS has advised that there was an undercount in 2001 care home resident statistics.
Left axis is care home population, right axis is total population.

Table 6 The percentage of people living in care homes by age group 1991/2001, by region

Region	1991 16–74	2001 16–74	1991 75–84	2001 75–84	1991 85+	2001 85+
North East	0.24	0.24	5.7	4.1	21.9	18.6
North West	0.27	0.21	6.2	3.9	24.7	17.9
Yorks and Humber	0.24	0.21	5.9	3.7	23.1	17.4
East Midlands	0.23	0.23	5.7	3.5	22.5	17.4
West Midlands	0.22	0.20	4.9	3.2	20.3	15.1
East	0.19	0.20	3.9	2.8	17.7	14.6
London	0.16	0.14	2.8	2.2	13.1	9.9
South East	0.30	0.25	4.7	3.3	23.1	17.2
South West	0.32	0.29	6.0	3.5	25.3	18.7
England	0.24	0.24	5.3	3.3	20.2	16.2
Scotland	0.15	0.21	3.9	4.0	16.9	17.7
Wales	0.24	0.20	6.4	3.2	21.6	15.6
Great Britain	0.23	0.23	5.1	3.4	20.0	16.3

Sources: Census Tables LBS04, ST126, ST232, SAS02, KS02.
Note: ONS has advised that there was an undercount in 2001 care home resident statistics.

Conclusion

In conclusion this chapter has demonstrated a large decline in local government care homes and national variation in the independent sector. The general trend is for a decline in the numbers of people below the age of 75 living in care homes. There has been an increase in the number of those over 85, and over 90, living in care homes, but, in general, rates of increase are below the rates of increase in the general older population of the UK.

In the next chapter the report examines the more detailed variations beneath this national picture by examining differences between local authorities.

3 Variations between local authority areas

Key findings

Much of this chapter is based on data for 'supported residents', that is, residents paid for by their local authority and resident either in the local authority area or in another area to which they have been 'exported'.

To summarise, we have found the following.

- In 2001, local authority areas exporting a high percentage of residents to other geographical local authority areas included, in particular, a number of Inner London boroughs.

- In 2001, data shows that the lowest ratios of supported residents to all residents were found in coastal areas. Care homes in such areas were likely to consist of relatively large numbers of incoming residents as well as higher proportions of private payers. These areas have still, however, been subject to a decline in care homes between 1991 and 2001.

- There were differences in the average percentage decline of care homes and care home residents in urban and rural/mixed areas. These were much greater if Wales was excluded.

- There was a difference in the average percentage of residents aged 75 and over living in care homes in 2001 in urban and rural/mixed areas.

- Coastal areas had the highest average proportion of older residents living in care homes and London boroughs the lowest.

- Changes in demography between 1991 and 2001 did not fully account for the differential rate of change in numbers of care home residents in areas classed either as urban or as rural/mixed. In particular, the differential rates of change in numbers of residents under 75 did not reflect demographic changes.

- In 2001, care home provision for older people was disproportionately concentrated in areas with the largest proportions of older people in the populations, which especially included coastal areas.

Variations between local authority areas

- In 2001, there tended to be a higher concentration of residential care provision for younger people in the same types of areas (particularly coastal) as residential care provision for older people.

- Local authority areas in Wales were untypical in that populations tended to comprise relatively high proportions of older people but low proportions living in care homes.

- Urban areas of England tended to have experienced greater levels of decline in residential/nursing care in the more deprived areas (i.e. areas that scored more highly on the deprivation index).

- 2001 Census health indicators suggest that residential care provision was often concentrated in places (largely rural/coastal areas) in which there may not have been the greatest need among older people.

- High property prices may have had a particular effect on the decline of care home provision in London, but they do not explain the higher rate of decline and relatively low level of provision in urban areas outside of London. However, data suggests that property prices may have had some effect on the rate of decline within Wales.

Supported residents in England and Wales

Figure 8 illustrates that supported places in care homes in England and Wales were still growing at the end of the 1990s. Supported places in local authority homes declined while supported places in the independent sector grew. This expenditure continued to represent a large proportion of the total public expenditure on all adult social care services throughout the decade. Department of Health (2002) statistics show that, in 2001, 46 per cent of all adult social care expenditure was spent on supporting residents in care homes and, for total expenditure on services for older people over 65, this proportion rose to 61 per cent.

Changes in communal provision for adult social care 1991–2001

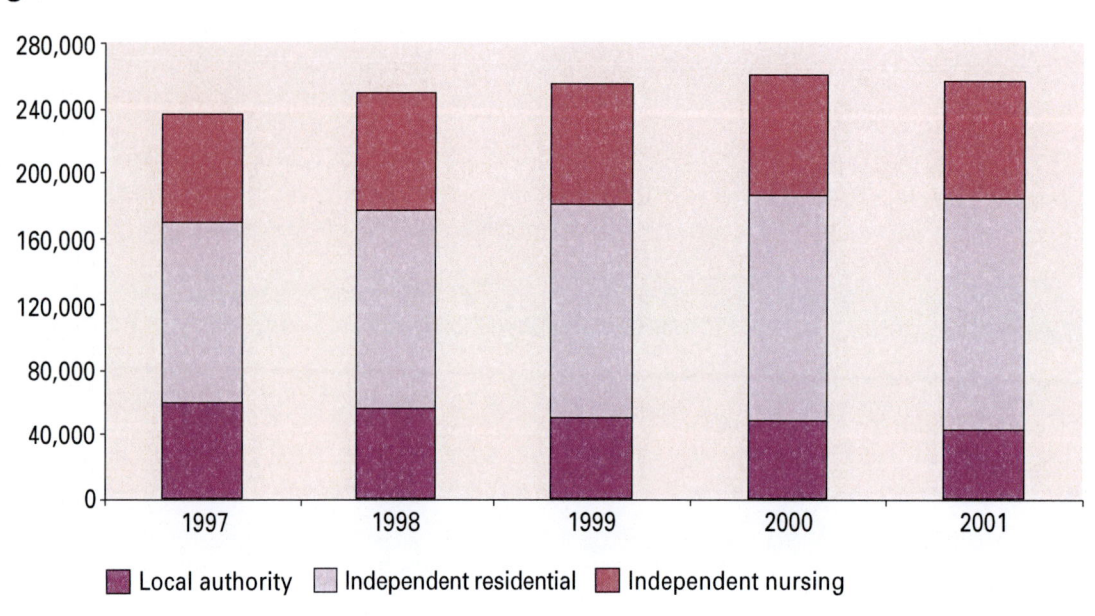

Figure 8 Local authority supported residents in residential and nursing care in England

■ Local authority □ Independent residential ■ Independent nursing

Source: Department of Health Statistics, 2003, Table C7.
Note: counts were dated at 31 March of each year.

Given the impact of this large amount of expenditure on the care home market, our research calculated the number of supported residents from each local area in 2001 in England and Wales.[1] As Scotland's financial support data is collated differently it was not possible to compare it with England and Wales, although it is discussed separately in the next section.

It was found that some local areas in England and Wales contained many more supported residents than care home residents living in that area, so this provided a good indication of the flow of supported residents out of area. The data could not estimate exactly where such residents go, but it provided an estimate of net outflow and conversely areas with low levels of state support. This is estimated by computing a ratio of supported residents to the number of care home residents living in the local authority area, where a value of greater than 1 indicates that an authority is supporting (exporting) more residents than it has living within its geographical boundaries.[2]

Table 7 identifies the English and Welsh 'exporting' local authorities in 2001. Table 8 shows the ten English authorities with the lowest levels of supported residents, i.e. where there is likely to be a larger market of individual private payers and some importing of supported residents. As illustrated in Figure 9, our analysis showed that most of these authorities were still subject to decline in residential care between 1991 and 2001, but that areas with the higher ratios of exported residents tended to

Variations between local authority areas

have experienced the greater levels of decline in total residents. The scatterplot highlights how this was particularly the case for Inner London boroughs. Areas with the smallest ratios are often associated anecdotally with retirement geography of England, including a number of key coastal towns and areas.

Table 7 Local authorities in England and Wales with ratios greater than 1 of local authority supported residents to total care home residents living in the area ('exporters'), 2001

Local authority	Number of supported residents	Number of care home residents in area	Ratio
Islington	1,067	206	5.2
Tower Hamlets	1,364	268	5.1
Westminster	1,113	221	5.0
Camden	1,082	283	3.8
Kensington & Chelsea	763	251	3.0
Hammersmith & Fulham	741	260	2.9
Hackney	1,095	387	2.8
Southwark	1,361	546	2.5
Newham	1,063	432	2.5
Haringey	1,176	480	2.5
Brent	1,150	566	2.0
Slough	481	247	1.9
Thurrock	458	241	1.9
Lambeth	1,534	873	1.8
Barking & Dagenham	919	540	1.7
St Helens	1,168	706	1.7
Lewisham	1,288	799	1.6
Hounslow	943	658	1.4
Hillingdon	1,076	753	1.4
Bexley	904	644	1.4
Nottingham	1,855	1,327	1.4
Wandsworth	1,405	1,006	1.4
Gateshead	1,465	1,097	1.3
Sheffield	4,272	3,210	1.3
Telford and Wrekin	839	632	1.3
Gwynedd	1,025	774	1.3
Salford	1,557	1,181	1.3
Luton	653	499	1.3
Newcastle-upon-Tyne	1,677	1,311	1.3
Kingston-upon-Hull	2,156	1,692	1.3
Rhondda, Cynon, Taff	1,343	1,062	1.3
Newport	814	669	1.2
Cardiff	1,452	1,204	1.2

(Continued)

Changes in communal provision for adult social care 1991–2001

Table 7 Local authorities in England and Wales with ratios greater than 1 of local authority supported residents to total care home residents living in the area ('exporters'), 2001 (Continued)

Local authority	Number of supported residents	Number of care home residents in area	Ratio
Calderdale	1,213	1,007	1.2
Merthyr Tydfil	338	281	1.2
Greenwich	1,030	862	1.2
Manchester	2,707	2,285	1.2
South Tyneside	1,313	1,111	1.2
Sandwell	1,823	1,566	1.2
Southampton	1,149	993	1.2
Liverpool	3,210	2,800	1.1
Birmingham	5,572	4,882	1.1
Leeds	4,280	3,764	1.1
Redbridge	953	840	1.1
Wigan	1,544	1,386	1.1
Wakefield	1,812	1634	1.1
Ealing	1,286	1168	1.1
Walsall	1,478	1353	1.1
Neath Port Talbot	875	802	1.1
Knowsley	709	667	1.1
Wolverhampton	1,296	1227	1.1

Sources: Department of Health Tables S3/6.12 (year to 31 March 2001), Census Table KS023.
Notes: ONS has advised there was an undercount in the 2001 resident care home statistics. Supported resident figures for Wales do not include respite care.

Table 8 Local authorities in England and Wales with the lowest ratios of supported funded residents to all care home residents living in the area, 2001

Local authority	Number of supported residents	Number of care home residents in area	Ratio
Bournemouth	1,023	2,655	0.39
Poole	504	1,223	0.41
Devon	3,243	7,852	0.41
East Sussex	2,973	7,076	0.42
Denbighshire/Sir Ddinbych	502	1,179	0.43
Wokingham	374	867	0.43
North Somerset	1,170	2,656	0.44
Torbay	946	2,107	0.45
Darlington	499	1,012	0.49
Southend	894	1,768	0.51

Sources: Department of Health Tables S3/6.12 (year to 31 March, 2001), Census Table KS023.
Notes: ONS has advised there was an undercount in the 2001 resident care home statistics. Supported resident figures for Wales do not include respite care.

Figure 9 Scatterplot showing the relationship between the percentage decline 1991–2001 in residents living in a local authority area and the ratio of local authority supported residents to total residents living in the area (by local authority in England and Wales)

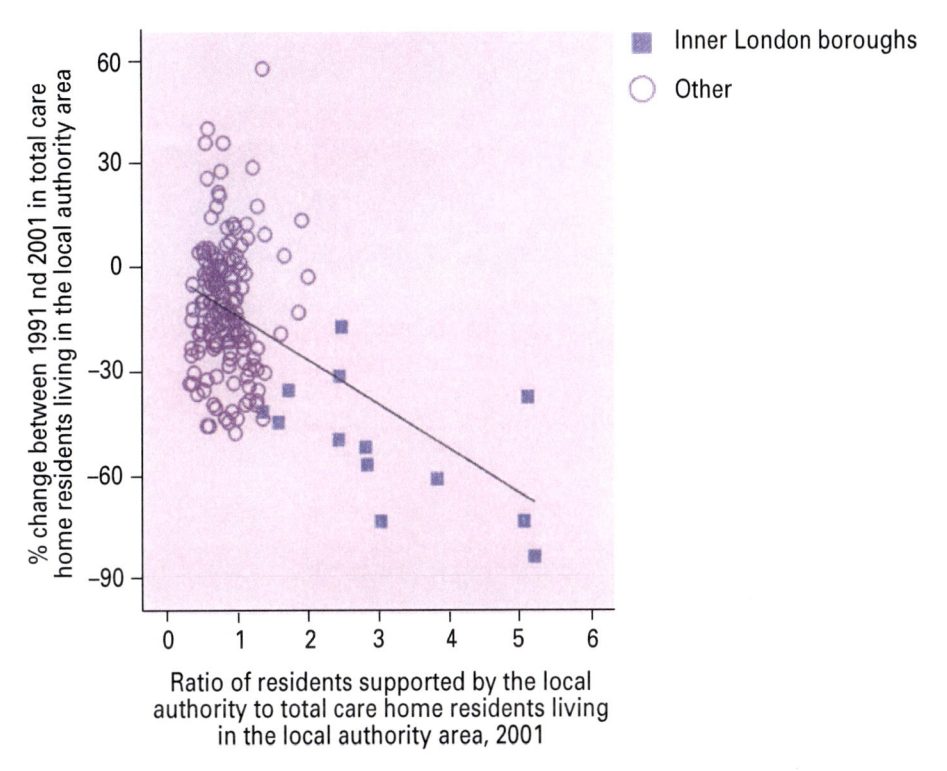

Sources: Department of Health Tables S3/6.12 (year to 31 March, 2001), Census Table KS023.
Notes: sig. (two tailed) <0.0005. R Squared Linear = 0.198.

Supported residents in Scotland

Table 9 shows the Scottish local authorities where the percentage of residents in the private and voluntary sector who are wholly or mainly funded by private means is above 40 per cent, indicating a larger proportion of individuals based in private sector homes in those areas.

Changes in communal provision for adult social care 1991–2001

Table 9 Financial support of residents in private and voluntary homes for older people in areas with high levels of private finance, Scotland, 2001

Local authority	Number wholly or mainly funded by private means	Percentage wholly or mainly funded by private means
Angus	358	56
Edinburgh, City of	567	55
Dumfries & Galloway	714	53
Moray	187	51
Perth & Kinross	479	49
Aberdeenshire	251	47
Midlothian	137	47
South Lanarkshire	450	47
Renfrewshire	161	46
Fife	581	45
Argyll & Bute	378	42
North Ayrshire	232	42
East Renfrewshire	158	41
Dundee City	219	40
Orkney Islands	20	40

Source: Scottish Executive Health Department Community Care Statistics, 2001.

Table 10 shows those Scottish local authorities areas with low levels of private funding and conversely more government funding activity across the sector. It is interesting to note that this includes a number of remote rural communities in addition to Glasgow.

Table 10 Financial support of residents in private and voluntary homes for older people in areas with low levels of private finance, Scotland, 2001

Local authority	Number wholly or mainly funded by private means	Percentage wholly or mainly funded by private means
Glasgow City	693	25
Scottish Borders	197	24
West Lothian	42	24
Clackmannanshire	9	22
North Lanarkshire	135	19
East Ayrshire	208	18
Eilean Siar (Western Isles)	20	15
Shetland Islands	64	5

Source: Scottish Executive Health Department Community Care Statistics, 2001.

Given the trend towards private sector care home provision between 1991 and 2001, and the general decline of the local authority sector, the distribution of supported funding within the private sector has become an important influence on policy and its management. The sector has complained that it is too dependent in many areas on the level of government funding, with an artificially low fixed price for contracted government-supported places. An independent report has criticised the 'two-tier system', whereby private residents pay much higher fees than those funded by local government support (Office of Fair Trading, 2005). This two-tier funding is likely to have affected the change in distribution of care homes between 1991 and 2001.

Local government performance

Our research included an analysis to see if changes in the local supply of residential care between 1991 and 2001 were associated with the performance management targets of local government in 2001. This analysis was for England only. Wales and Scotland use a different and independent approach to the setting of performance targets.

In 2001 the key performance indicator for social care for adult services was the number of admissions of older people to emergency health care per 1,000 in the population. There were, however, methodological difficulties with focusing on this indicator in local government areas because of its computation by the NHS in health authority areas. The geography of health authority areas was not always coterminous with local government authorities. As a result, a similar variable of the number of all emergency admissions to hospital per 1,000 in the population has been made available for all local authority social care areas in England, but this contains all adults, not just those aged 65 and over.

There is no area association between English local authority performance scores in the amount of emergency admissions and the change in number of social care homes in local areas between 1991 and 2001. In other words, a reduction in social care homes does not appear to lead to a higher level of emergency admissions in that area. The relationship of the rate of emergency admissions in a local area is likely to be associated with a complex range of factors, including area deprivation and provision rates of a range of services, including community care and home support services.

The research also examined another key performance indicator of less political importance in 2001. This was a local government 'best value' indicator: 'the proportion of older people, aged 65 and over, helped to live at home'. This indicator

Changes in communal provision for adult social care 1991–2001

includes both low-level care and intensive home care. Satisfactory performance is defined as above 60 cases per 1,000 in the local population. Across England there was no general association between good performance and a decline in the number of care homes available between 1991 and 2001. But, when English local authorities were grouped into those that export a surplus of care home residents to other local areas and those that do not (using the classification in Table 7 above), it was found that there was a significant difference between the two groups. The exporting areas had a better average on the performance score of 106 per 1,000 compared to the score of 86 per 1,000 for the other group. The England average was 84 per 1,000. We can conclude that these exporting areas, such as those in Inner London (Table 7), are more likely to have higher levels of older people helped to live at home. But it is important to note that this effect might be caused by the higher number of poorer older people living in urban areas and approaching government care services, whereas wealthy older people living in non-urban areas are more likely to make their own arrangement with private services without seeking local government help. In conclusion there is no strong association between an area's performance on government targets and its level of social care home closure between 1991 and 2001.

Political control and change in urban areas

Our analysis explored the hypothesis that Conservative-controlled authorities were keener privatisers than others. Only the English metropolitan boroughs (i.e. 68 districts in London, Greater Manchester, South Yorkshire, West Yorkshire, Merseyside, Tyne and Wear and West Midlands) were included in the test sample, as these areas had been unaffected by boundary changes, allowing the two election years (1990/1998) to be compared.

The mean average of decline in local authority homes between 1991 and 2001 was examined by local political control in 1990, the hypothesis being that Conservative control in 1990 would lead to greater decline. Results showed a higher rate of decline of local authority owned homes in those boroughs that were Conservative ($M = -70$ per cent) controlled in 1990, than was the case in Labour ($M = -54$ per cent) or other ($M = -53$ per cent) constituencies. The difference between the mean averages for Conservative and Labour areas ($U = 192$, $p = 0.05$) was statistically significant. The distribution of the percentage changes in residents for both groups is illustrated in Figure 10. Each box contains 50 per cent of the percentages and the protruding lines represent the full range from the lowest to the highest percentage. The black lines represent the median average. Outliers are shown by the circles and stars (extreme cases).

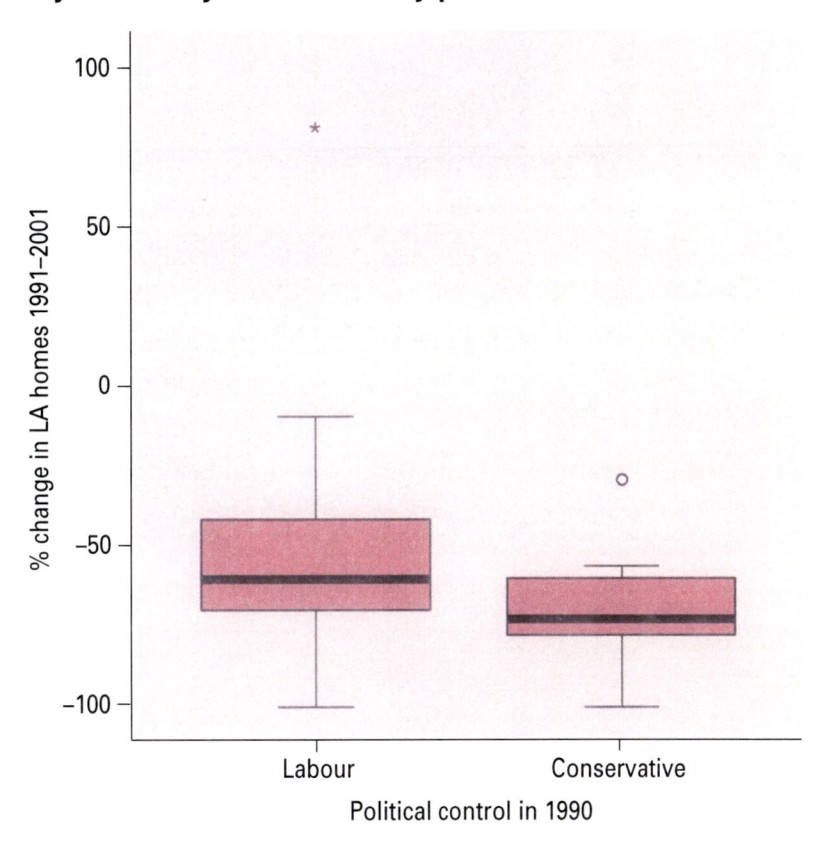

Figure 10 Boxplot showing the range and median average of percentage change in local authority homes by local authority political control

[Boxplot: Y-axis "% change in LA homes 1991–2001" from -100 to 100; X-axis "Political control in 1990" with categories Labour and Conservative]

Sources: Rallings and Thrasher (1999) Census Tables SAS03, UV70, KS023.

These results suggest that political control may have had a small effect on the decline of local authority residential care in urban areas. It was not possible to test whether political control had any effect on the different trends identified in rural and urban areas (as discussed below). This was because all the local authorities included in the sample were urban boroughs (as counties were not included because of the complications of boundary changes). Results should therefore be viewed with caution due to the unrepresentative nature of the sample, which was exclusively urban and therefore predominately Labour controlled.

Variations by area classification

In order to examine the relationship between changes in communal care and type of area (i.e. whether urban or rural), a basic classification was applied to local authority areas of either 'urban' or 'rural/mixed'.[3] It was then tested to see whether there were any significant differences between the two categories in terms of changes in

Changes in communal provision for adult social care 1991–2001

numbers of care homes and residents, and in the proportion of people in the population living in such establishments. A more detailed area classification system[4] was also used for analysis of 2001 data on the proportion of older people living in care homes.

Findings suggest that different patterns of change were evident in rural and urban areas. The mean average decline in urban areas was −6.7 per cent for homes and −14.9 per cent for residents, while in rural/mixed areas there was an increase of 4.5 per cent for homes and 3.6 per cent for residents. The average percentage increase in rural/mixed areas was much greater if Welsh districts were excluded, as the large decline in Wales was not typical of rural areas. If Wales was included, however, differences in the mean averages in urban and rural/mixed areas were only found to be statistically significant for local authority care. The independent sector saw average increases for homes and residents in both the urban and the rural/mixed group, and, although these were larger for the rural/mixed areas, the difference was not found to be statistically significant. The distribution of the percentage changes in residents for both groups is illustrated in Figure 11.

Figure 11 Boxplot showing the range and median average of percentage change in total residents by type of area, 1991–2001

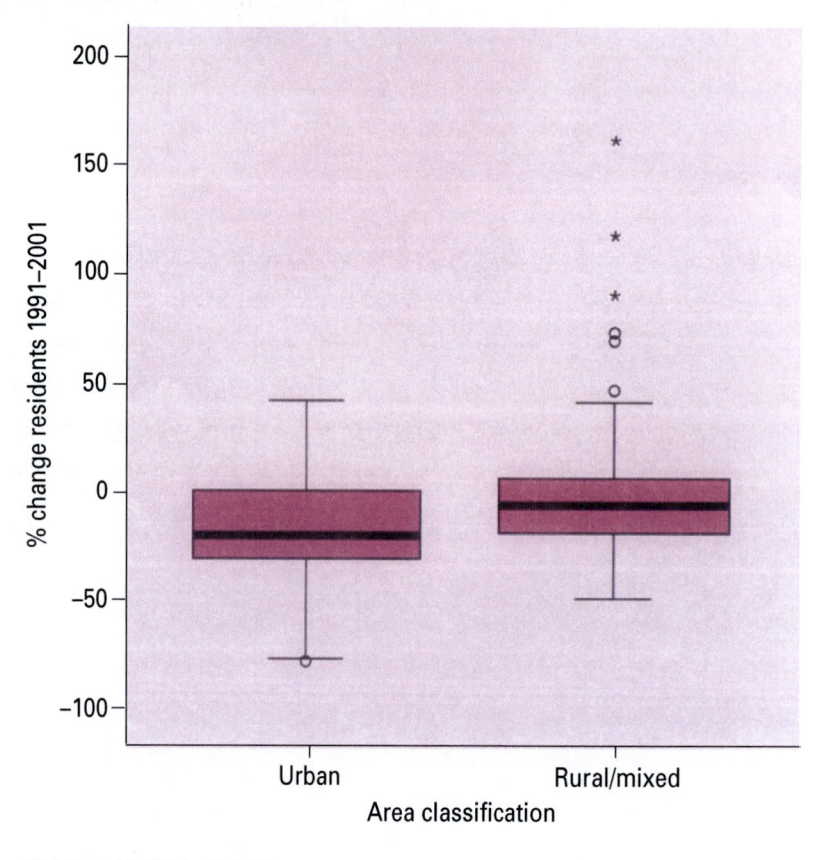

Sources: Census Tables SAS03, KS023.

Variations between local authority areas

Findings also show that, for both types of area, there was a difference in the average percentage of people aged 75 and over living in care homes. This was true for both years. In 1991, the mean average for urban areas was 7.7 per cent. This had declined to 5.9 per cent in 2001. For rural/mixed areas the average had also declined, but for both years remained higher than the urban averages, at 8.4 per cent and 6.9 per cent respectively. The increase in the difference between the averages meant that this had become statistically significant by 2001.

For 2001, the average proportion of older people living in care homes was identified for five types of area. This is illustrated in Figure 12, which shows that districts of a rural (M = 7.4 per cent), and in particular coastal, character (M = 7.8 per cent) had comparatively high proportions of older people (75+) living in care homes. In the classification system used,[5] coastal areas were divided into three types. Of these it was evident that the average proportion of older people in care homes was significantly higher in 'coastal resorts' (M = 9.7 per cent) than in those described as 'aged coastal resorts' (M = 7.5 per cent) (many of which are identified as in decline as resorts) and 'aged coastal extremities' (M = 7.3 per cent) (i.e. coastal areas that are much more rural in character). The 'mixed' group shown in Figure 12 combined the sub-groups 'mixed urban' and 'typical towns', which were included in the 'rural' family but described as 'neither totally urban nor completely rural' (Office of Fair Trading, 2005, p. 51). The average was actually slightly lower for the 'mixed' districts (M = 6.3) than for the 'urban other' group (M = 6.6) but, as is shown in the boxplot, there was much more variation in the mixed group than for any of the others (SD = 2.2). The lowest average proportion by far was evident for the London districts (M = 3.7 per cent).

The 2001 geographical differences in the proportions of older people living in care homes are also illustrated in Figures 13 and 14. Figure 13 shows the areas surrounding the capital to have had relatively low proportions of older people living in care homes and highlights the comparatively high proportions in many coastal areas. The relatively low proportions in many of the Welsh counties are also notable. The London map in Figure 14 highlights the lower proportions of older people in care homes in many of the Inner London boroughs (many of which have been identified in Table 7 earlier in this chapter as major 'exporters').

Changes in communal provision for adult social care 1991–2001

Figure 12 Boxplot showing the range and median average percentage of older people living in care homes by type of area, 2001

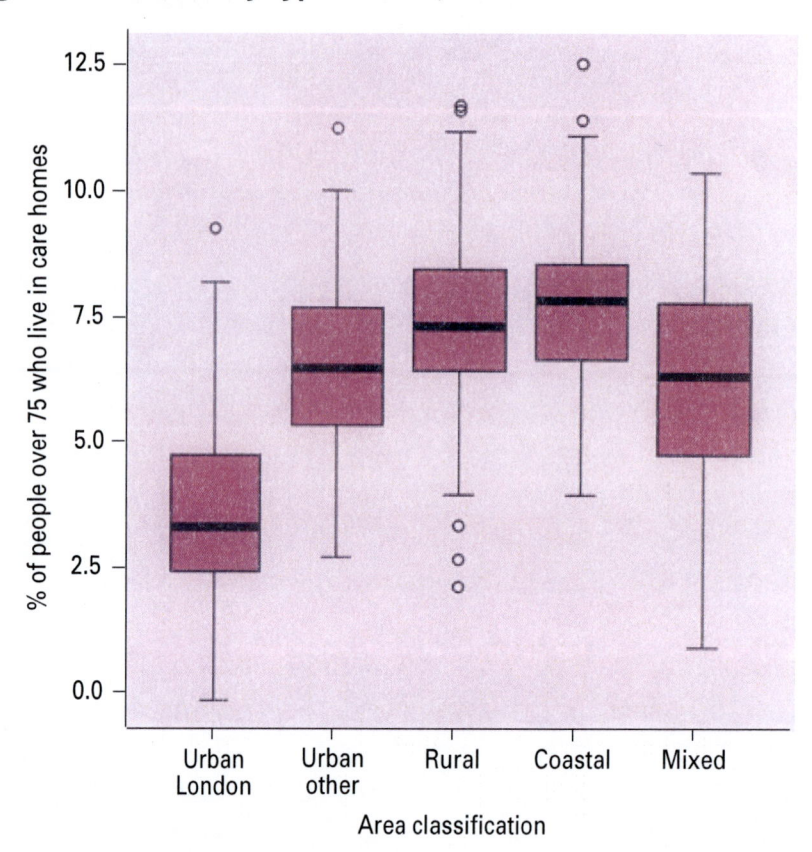

Sources: Census Tables: ST126, ST232, KS02.
Classification derived from Vickers, D., Rees, P. and Birkin, M. (2003) *A New Classification of UK Local Authorities Using 2001 Census Key Statistics*, University of Leeds.

Variations between local authority areas

Figure 13 UK map showing the proportion of people aged 75 and over living in care homes in each district, 2001

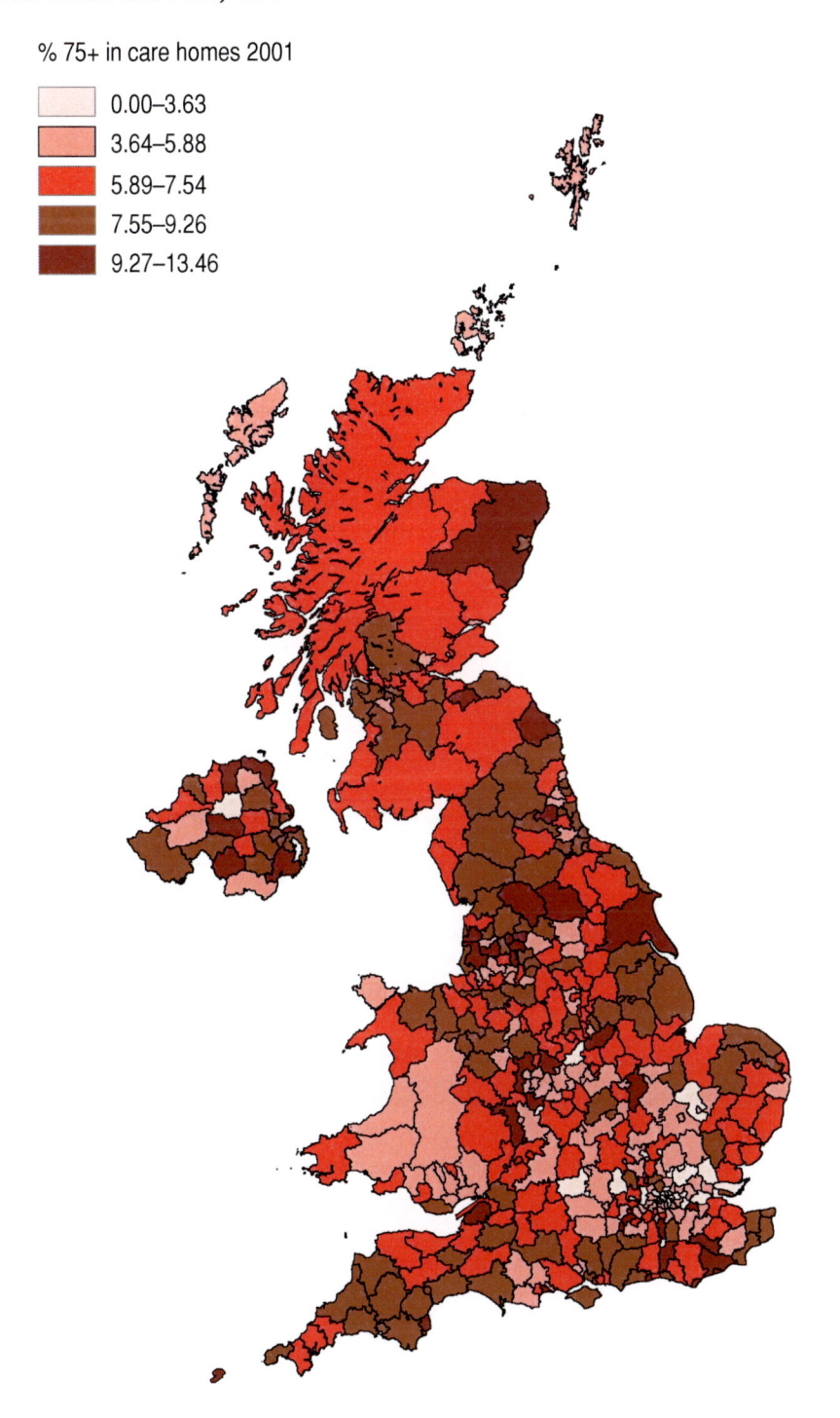

% 75+ in care homes 2001
- 0.00–3.63
- 3.64–5.88
- 5.89–7.54
- 7.55–9.26
- 9.27–13.46

Sources: Census Tables KS02, ST126, ST232, ST301.
Note: for a discussion of Northern Ireland data see Appendix 1.

Changes in communal provision for adult social care 1991–2001

Figure 14 London map showing the proportion of people aged 75 and over living in care homes in each district, 2001

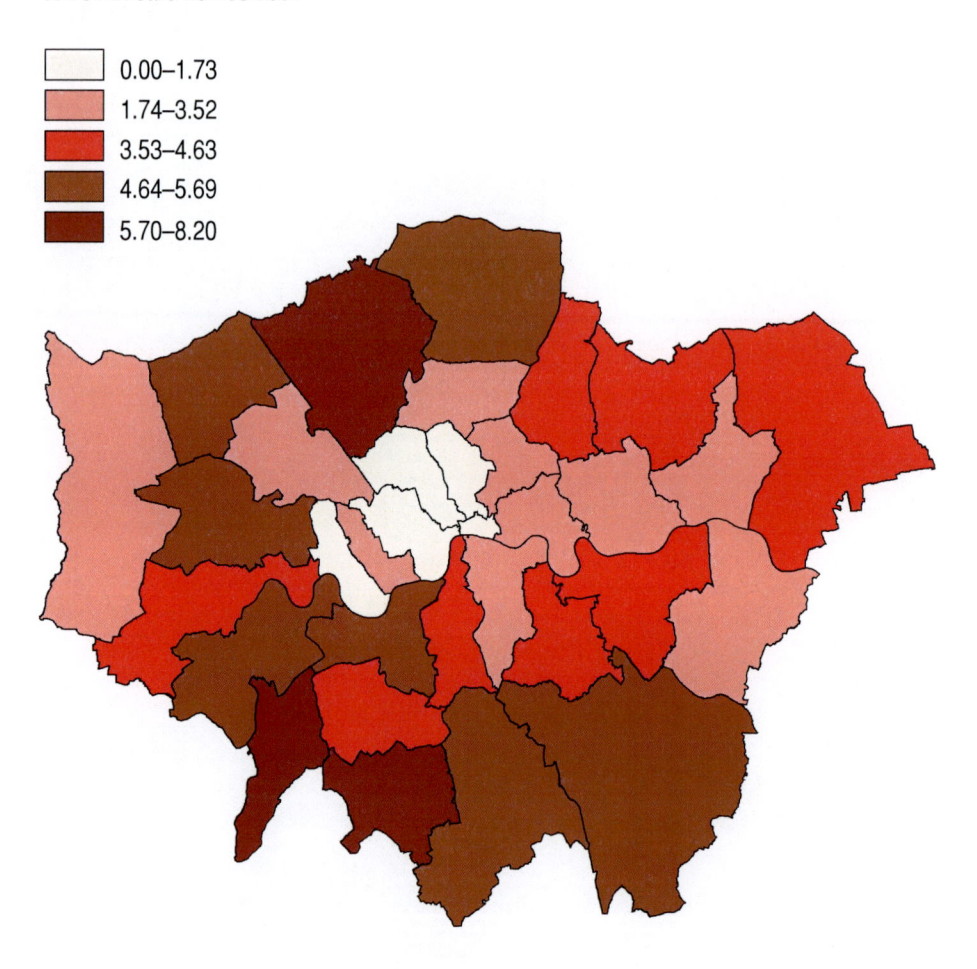

% 75+ in care homes 2001

- 0.00–1.73
- 1.74–3.52
- 3.53–4.63
- 4.64–5.69
- 5.70–8.20

Sources: Census Tables KS02, ST126, ST232.

Demography

An important question in relation to these changes was whether, and to what extent, they were linked to demographic trends. In particular, was the increase in residents in rural/mixed areas related to a greater proportionate increase in the number of older people in these areas? This question was addressed by comparing the change between 1991 and 2001 in the number of people aged 75 and over by area, with the change in the number of care home residents in the same age group by area. Findings, however, suggest that this link was not very strong. The association between the percentage change in the 75 and over total population and the 75 and over care home population, was only statistically significant in urban areas. Figures 15a and b show that in both cases there was a positive association between the two variables, but Figure 15b shows that in rural/mixed areas this was particularly weak. It should also be noted that there was a significant difference in the average percentage change in care home residents aged under 75 in the two types of area, which did not reflect corresponding demographic changes.[6]

Figure 15a Scatterplot showing the relationship between changes in the 75 and over total population and the 75 and over care home population in urban local authority areas, 1991–2001

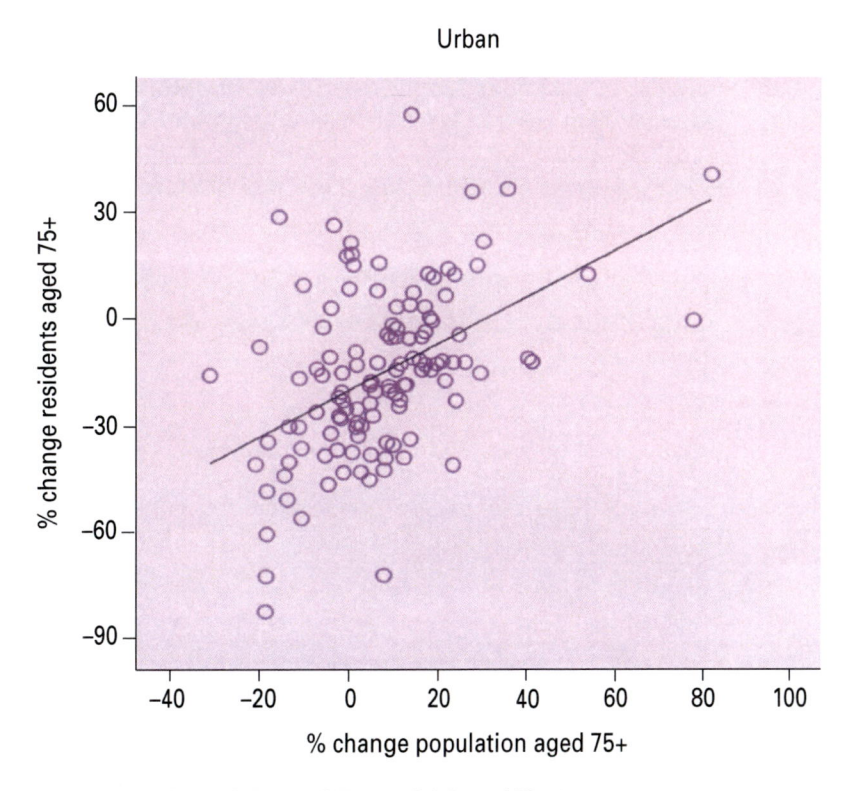

Sources: Census Tables LBS04, ST126, ST232, SAS02, KS02.
R Squared Linear = 0.225.

Changes in communal provision for adult social care 1991–2001

Figure 15b Scatterplot showing the relationship between changes in the 75 and over total population and the 75 and over care home population in rural/mixed local authority areas, 1991–2001

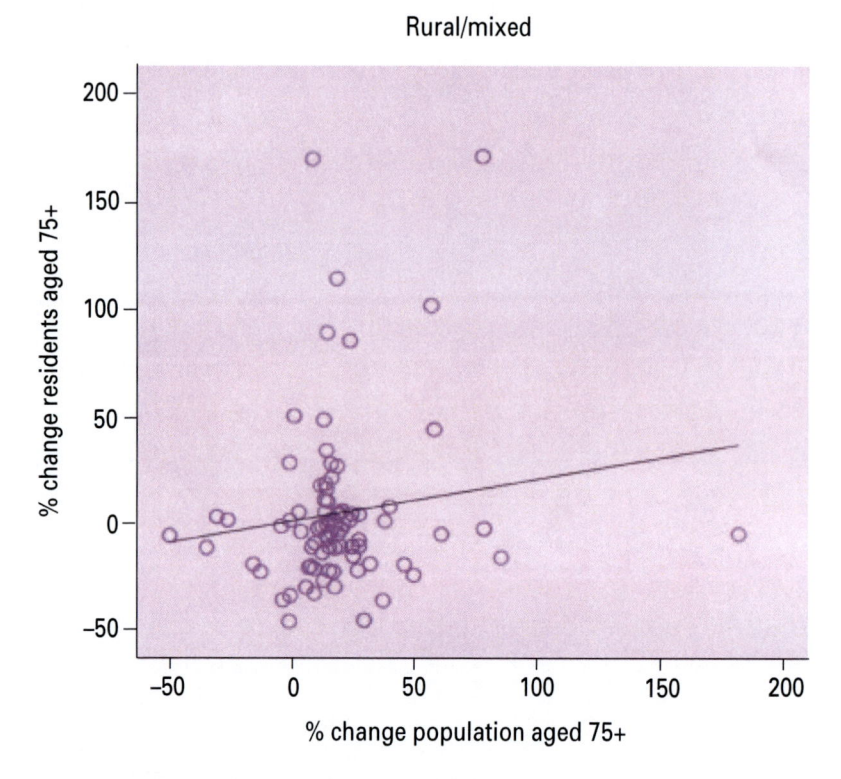

Sources: Census Tables LBS04, ST126, ST232, SAS02, KS02.
R Squared Linear = 0.02.

The UK map in Figure 16 if compared with Figure 13 earlier in this chapter shows that not all areas with higher proportions of older people in the populations had higher proportions of older people in care homes (in 2001). In particular this is notable in Wales, which had on average the highest proportion of people aged 75 and over in the population (M = 8.4 per cent) of any region except the South West of England (M = 9.2 per cent), but had a relatively low average proportion of older people living in care homes (M = 6.3 per cent, overall M = 6.5 per cent).

The two UK maps (Figures 16 and 17) also show that many district areas in the North West also stand out from this pattern, having high proportions in care homes in areas with relatively young populations. In addition, the London map in Figure 17 if compared with Figure 14 earlier in the chapter shows that there was not (in 2001) a direct correlation between the two variables. For example, it highlights how some of the Outer London boroughs such as Bexley and Barking and Dagenham had the highest proportions of people aged 75 and over, yet had low proportions of these older people living in care homes.

Variations between local authority areas

Figure 16 UK map showing the proportion of people aged 75 and over in the population of each district, 2001

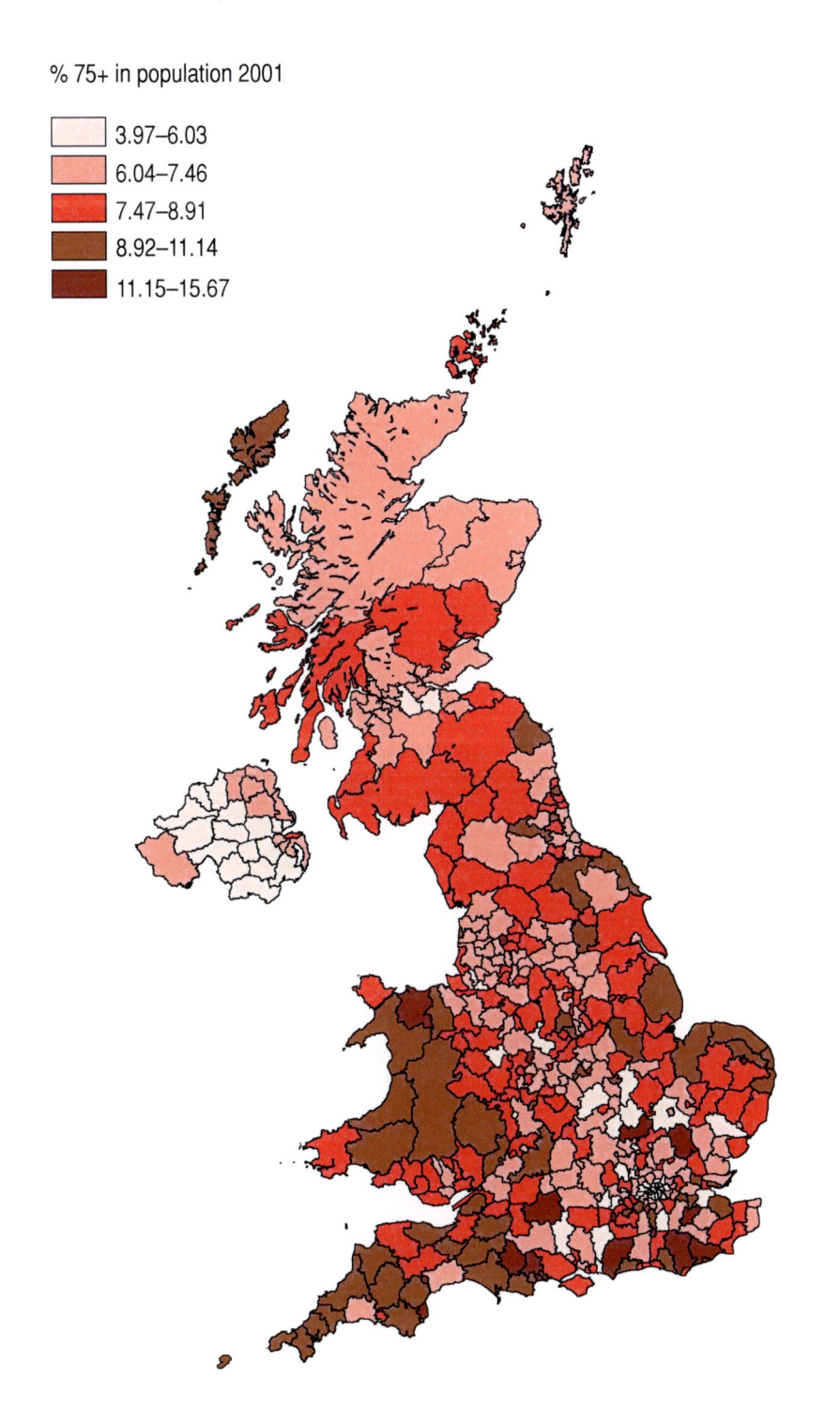

% 75+ in population 2001

- 3.97–6.03
- 6.04–7.46
- 7.47–8.91
- 8.92–11.14
- 11.15–15.67

Source: Census Table KS02.
Note: for a discussion of Northern Ireland data see Appendix 1.

Changes in communal provision for adult social care 1991–2001

Figure 17 London map showing the proportion of people aged 75 and over in each district, 2001

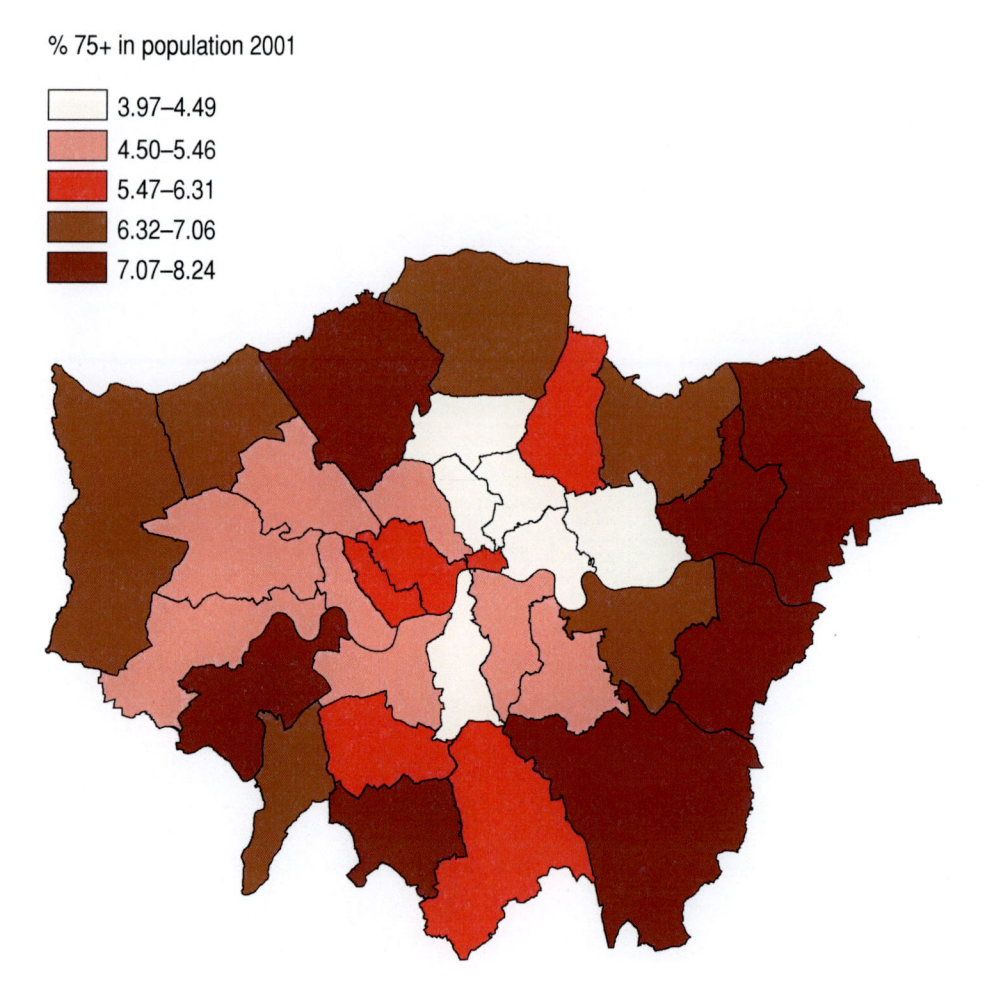

% 75+ in population 2001
- 3.97–4.49
- 4.50–5.46
- 5.47–6.31
- 6.32–7.06
- 7.07–8.24

Source: Census Table KS02.

Variations between local authority areas

Despite these exceptions, Figure 18 shows that, in 2001, there was an overall association between the size of the older population in an area and the proportion of older people living in care homes, i.e. a person aged 75+ was more likely to live in a care home, the larger the proportion of older people in the area in which s/he was living. It also highlights the relationship between these variables and area type. In particular, coastal areas stand out as on average having had both a high proportion of people aged 75+ in the population and a high proportion of aged 75+ living in care homes, while the reverse is seen to have been the case for the London boroughs. Figure 19 shows that residential and nursing care for under 75s also tends to be concentrated in the same types of areas as care for older people, i.e. being most prevalent in coastal areas and least so in London authorities.

Figure 18 Scatterplot showing the relationship between the proportionate size of the 75+ total population and the proportion of people aged 75+ living in care homes, by type of local authority area, 2001

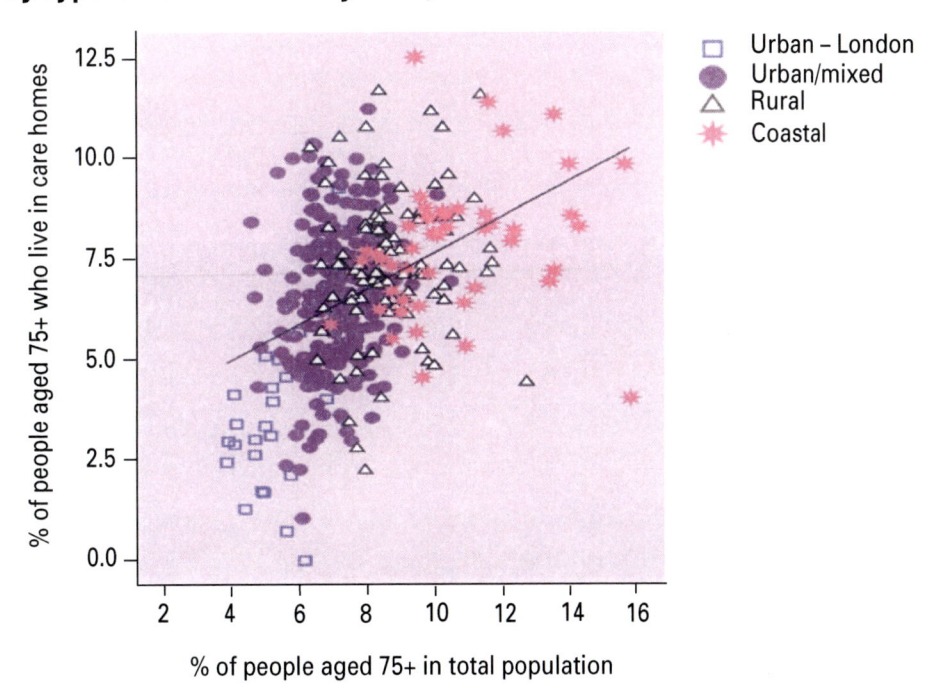

Sources: KS02, ST126, ST232.[7]
Notes: sig. (two tailed) <0.0005. Includes all district areas in Great Britain. R Squared Linear = 0.16.

Changes in communal provision for adult social care 1991–2001

Figure 19 Scatterplot showing the relationship between the proportion of people aged 16–74 living in care homes and the proportion of people aged 75+ living in care homes, by type of local authority area, 2001

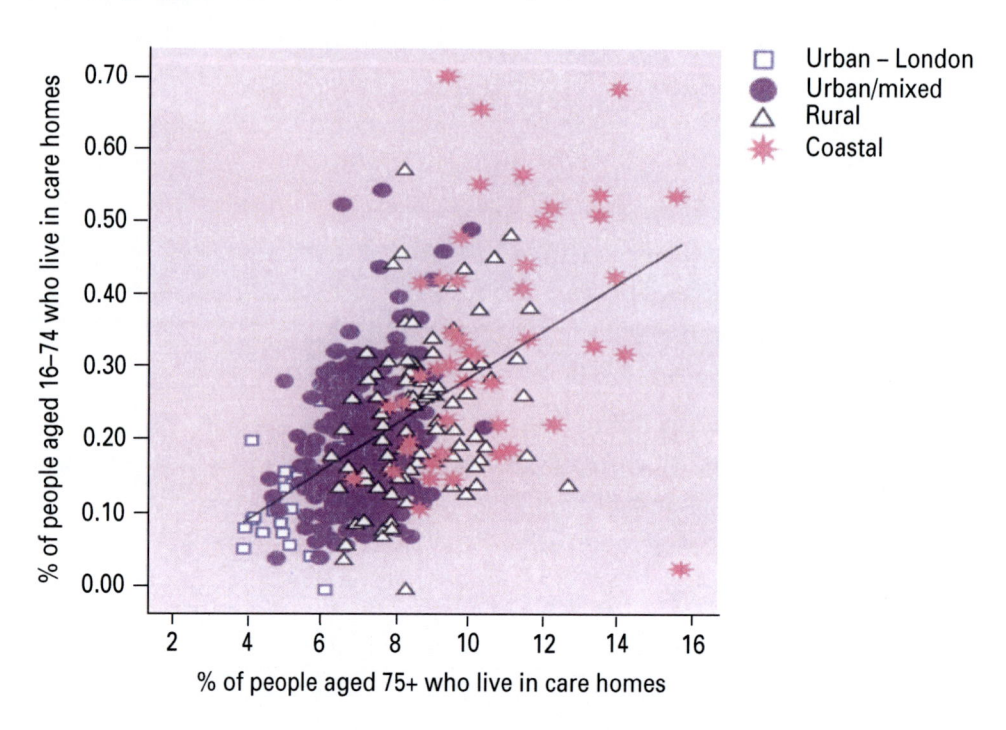

Sources: KS02, ST126, ST232.[8]
Notes: sig. (two tailed) <0.0005. Includes all district areas in Great Britain. R Squared Linear = 0.255.

Poverty and health indicators

Urban local authority areas ($M = 25.9$) tended to score more highly than rural/mixed areas ($M = 15.5$) on the deprivation index. As older people in urban areas were less likely to be living in residential or nursing care, this suggests that poorer sections of the population were likely to have been under-represented in care homes. Census data on the percentage change in care home residents was plotted against indices of deprivation in order to explore associations between these two factors. As shown in Figure 20, the more deprived an area was on the indices of deprivation the greater the decline in residential and nursing care, i.e. there was a negative association between the deprivation scores for English authorities and the percentage change in care home residents. Among the English local authority areas there was a negative association in both urban and rural/mixed areas (but this was only statistically significant in urban areas).[9] There was no association between deprivation scores and the percentage change of care home residents in Scotland and Wales.[10]

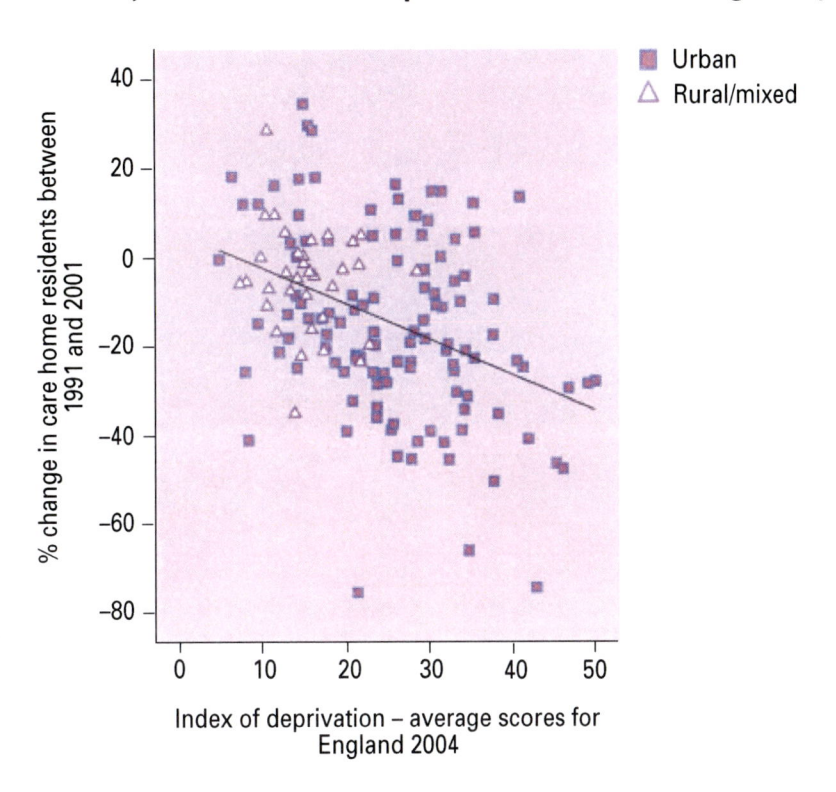

Figure 20 Scatterplot showing the relationship between the percentage change in care home residents, 1991–2001 and deprivation scores for England (2004)

Sources: Census Tables SAS03, KS023/Office of the Deputy Prime Minister.
Note: sig. (two tailed) <0.0005. R Squared Linear = 0.159.

Findings also showed that there was a negative association between the proportion of older people in care homes and deprivation scores, i.e. the more deprived the area, the less likely an older person was to be living in a care home. However, this association was not statistically significant for local authority areas in England ($r = -0.148$, $p = 0.71$), unless those in the North East region (which had some very high deprivation scores and a high proportion of people aged 75 and over living in care homes) were excluded from the analysis. But, even then, the association remained weak ($r = -0.199$, $p = 0.20$). There were also negative associations in Scotland and Wales but again these were very weak and not statistically significant.[11]

Findings for 2001 showed that areas with a larger proportion of older people in households reporting to have a limiting long-term illness and 'not good health' tended to have lower proportions of older people living in care homes. This is illustrated in Figure 21 (if compared with the UK map in Figure 13 earlier in this chapter), which, for example, shows a high proportion of older people with poor health in districts in South Wales (where proportionately few older people were living in care homes) and low proportions of older people having poor health in many coastal areas (where there are comparatively high levels of residential care).[12]

Changes in communal provision for adult social care 1991–2001

Figure 21 UK map showing the proportion of people aged 75 and over reporting to have both a 'limiting long-term illness' and 'not good health', 2001

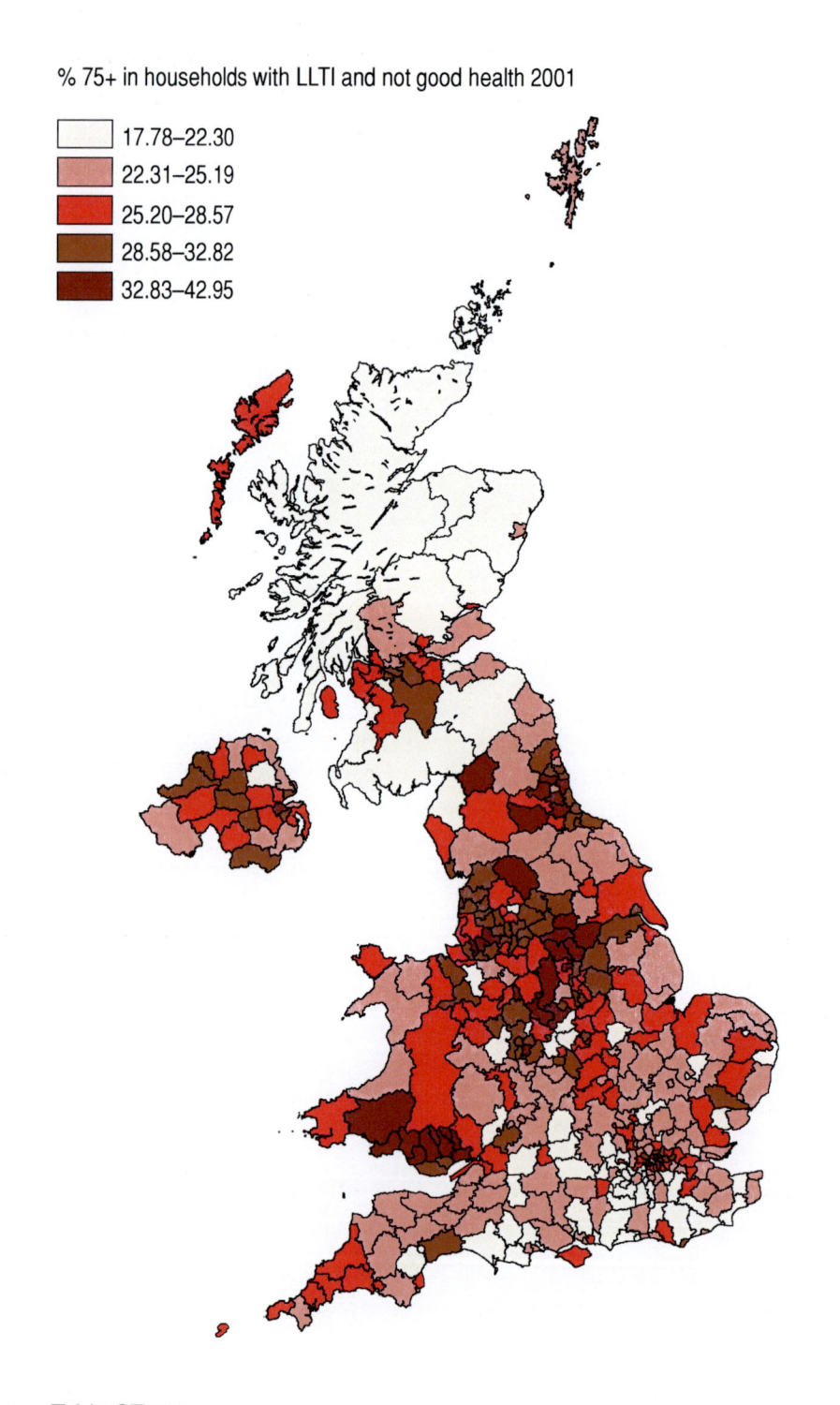

% 75+ in households with LLTI and not good health 2001

- 17.78–22.30
- 22.31–25.19
- 25.20–28.57
- 28.58–32.82
- 32.83–42.95

Source: Census Table ST106.
Note: for a discussion of Northern Ireland data see Appendix 1.

Variations between local authority areas

Similarly, Figure 22 if compared with Figure 14 earlier in this chapter shows that some of the boroughs in South London (in particular Sutton and Kingston upon Thames) had smaller proportions of older people in households with relatively poor health, while having comparatively larger proportions of older people living in care homes. In addition, the five boroughs marked with the darkest shade (for 29.31–34.7 per cent) in Figure 22, forming a band across to East London from Islington to Barking and Dagenham, are shown in Figure 14 to have low proportions of older people living in care homes.

Data also showed that there was a significant difference in the average proportion of older people that reported to have a 'limiting long-term illness' and 'not good health' in urban ($M = 19.3$) and rural/mixed local authority areas ($M = 17.0$).[13] The negative association between the proportion of older people with a 'limiting long-term illness' (LLTI) and 'not good health' and the proportion living in care homes in 2001, however, was not statistically significant ($r = -0.014$, $p = 0.772$).

The extent to which the poorer sections of the population (who were also more likely to have poor health) were under-represented in care homes was impossible to assess, as we could not know how many people in need of residential care were 'exported' from urban to rural areas. Figure 23, however, suggests that the ratios of local authority supported residents to all residents in the area were on average significantly greater in urban than rural/mixed areas, indicating that local authorities in urban areas are more likely to export residents, while residents in rural areas are more likely to have been 'imported' from other authorities (and/or to be private payers). Therefore it could be that people in urban areas were not necessarily less likely to enter residential care, but they were less likely to enter a care home in their own area – a factor that may be more likely to impact on poorer sections of the population for whom moving out of their area may be more difficult.

Changes in communal provision for adult social care 1991–2001

Figure 22 London map showing the proportion of people aged 75 and over reporting to have both a 'limiting long-term illness' and 'not good health', 2001

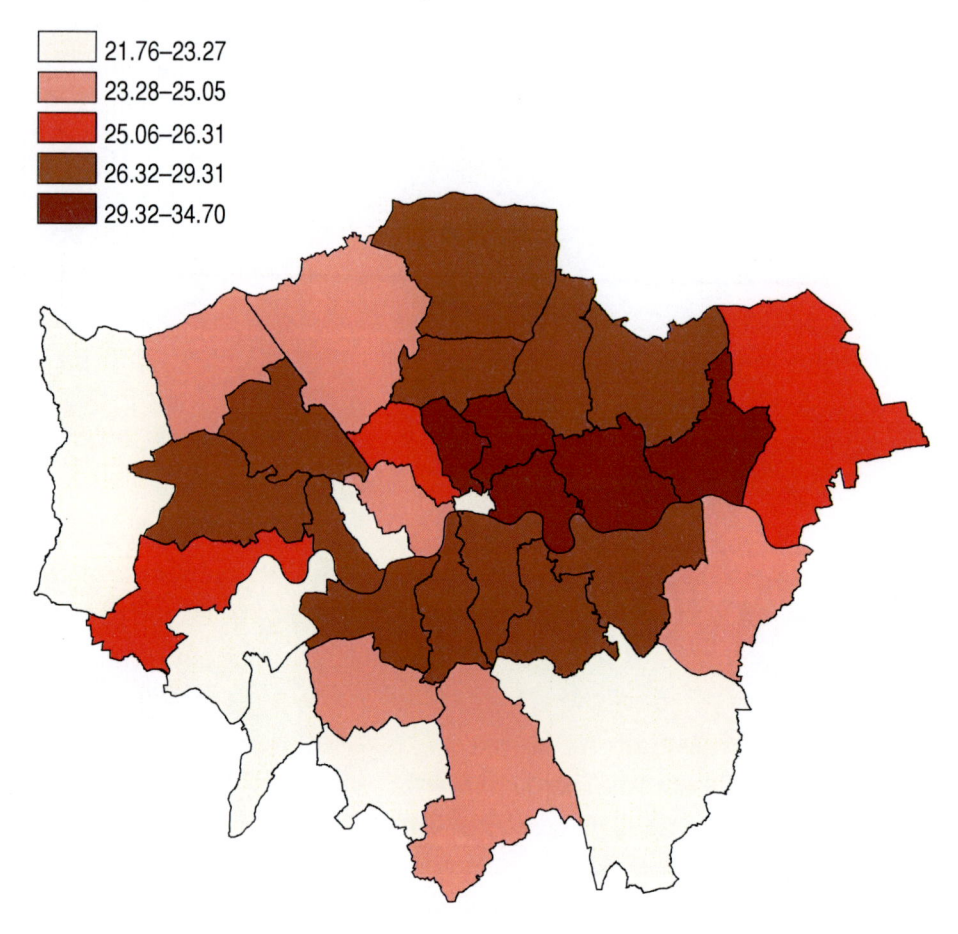

% 75+ in households with LLTI and not good health 2001

- 21.76–23.27
- 23.28–25.05
- 25.06–26.31
- 26.32–29.31
- 29.32–34.70

Source: Census Table ST106.

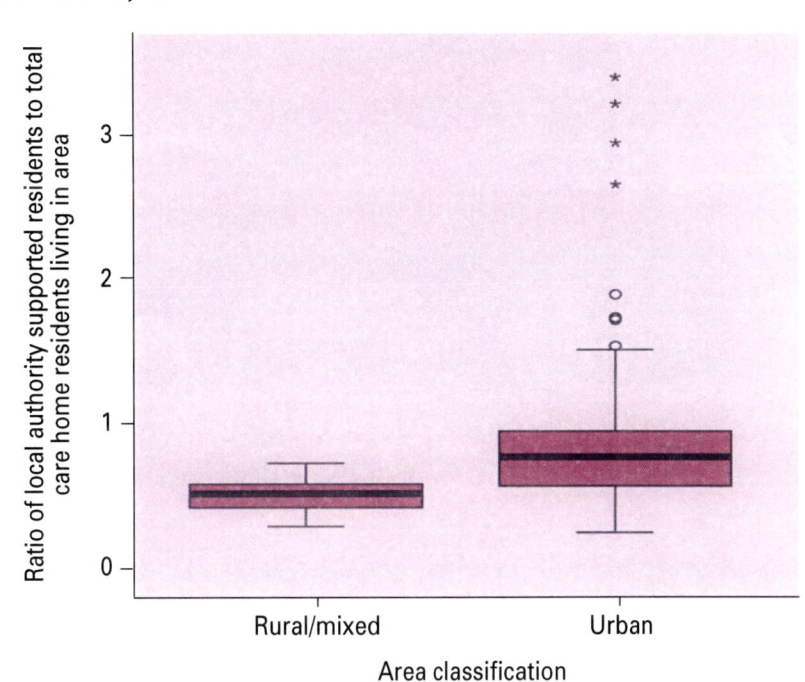

Figure 23 Box plot showing the range and median average in the ratio of local authority supported residents to total care home residents (in England and Wales) by area classification, 2001

[Box plot showing Ratio of local authority supported residents to total care home residents living in area, by Area classification (Rural/mixed and Urban)]

Sources: Department of Health Tables S3/6.12 (year to 31 March 2001); Census Table KS023.
Note: independent t-test result: urban: ($M = 0.9$, SD = 0.5); rural/mixed: ($M = 0.5$, SD = 0.1) $t(139) = -6.8$, $p < 0.0005$.

Property prices

Another variable investigated was property prices. The question was asked whether differences in property prices had any influence on changes in the provision of residential and nursing care. Changes in property prices were therefore correlated against changes in the number of care homes, both at regional and local authority area level for England and Wales, but not for Scotland (where comparable data was not available).

Findings showed no association between the percentage change in average regional house prices and the percentage change in residential care homes ($r = -0.180$, $p = 0.597$). If non-local-authority homes were not included there was, however, a stronger negative association ($r = -0.576$, $p = 0.063$), although this was only statistically significant if Scotland was excluded from the analysis (in which case $r = -0.633$, $p = 0.049$).

When average house prices (for local authority areas of England and Wales, 2001) were plotted against percentage increase in the number of homes, a weak negative association was found ($r = -0.173$, $p = 0.024$). There was, however, a stronger negative relationship between higher house prices and the percentage increase in

Changes in communal provision for adult social care 1991–2001

total homes within some specific regions (see Figure 24). In London and Wales (see Figure 25 for an illustration of the Welsh association), higher average house prices in a local area were associated with a greater percentage decline in the number of homes in that area between 1991 and 2001.

The resulting situation in 2001 was also explored in terms of looking at the relationship between average house prices and the proportion of older people in care homes in 2001 by local authority area. As is shown in Figure 24, there was also a statistically significant association between the two variables ($r = -0.494$, $p = <0.0005$). However, this is largely resulting from the situation in London, with its particularly high average house prices and low proportion of older people in residential or nursing care. If London is removed there is no association ($r = 0.061$, $p = 0.471$). If all local authority areas are included there is a statistically significant difference ($p = 0.023$) between the mean average house price in 'urban' ($M = £109,048$) and 'rural/mixed' ($M = £91,753$) areas. However, without London, this is no longer the case, as the majority of urban areas are in the North where house prices were on average comparatively low. Therefore, higher property prices cannot account for the relatively low (although higher than in London) level of residential and nursing care in urban areas outside of London.

Figure 24 Scatterplot showing the relationship between the proportion of over 75s living in care homes (2001) and house prices in England (2000), by local authority area

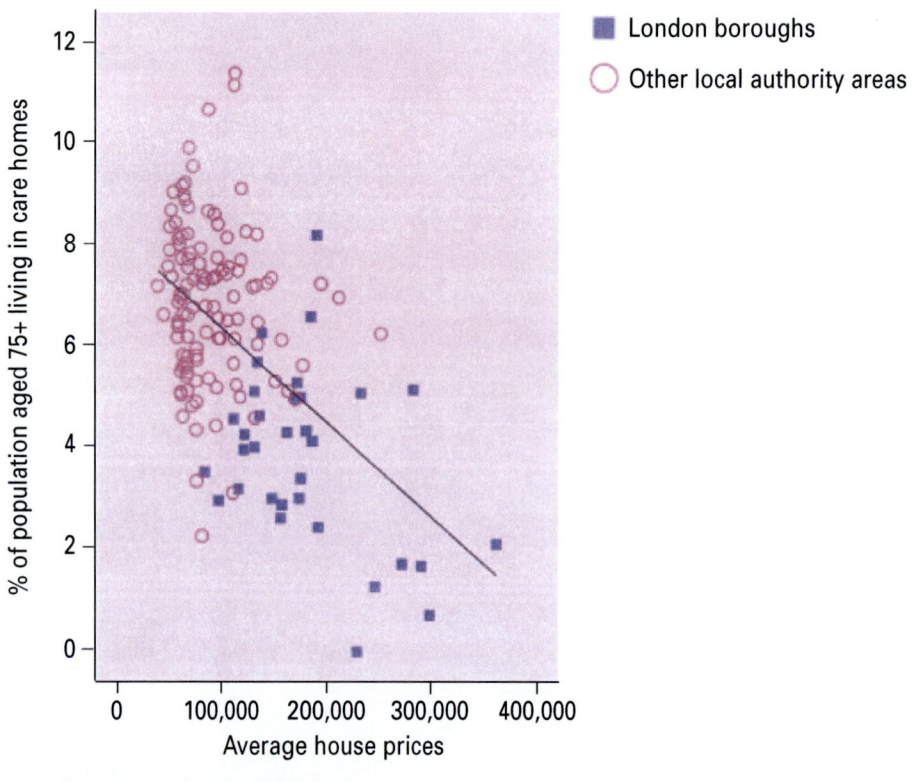

Sources: Land Registry, Census Tables ST126, ST232, KS02.
Note: $p < 0.0005$. R Squared Linear = 0.278.

Variations between local authority areas

Figure 25 Scatterplot showing the relationship between the percentage change in care homes (1991–2001), and house prices in Wales (2000), by Welsh local authority area

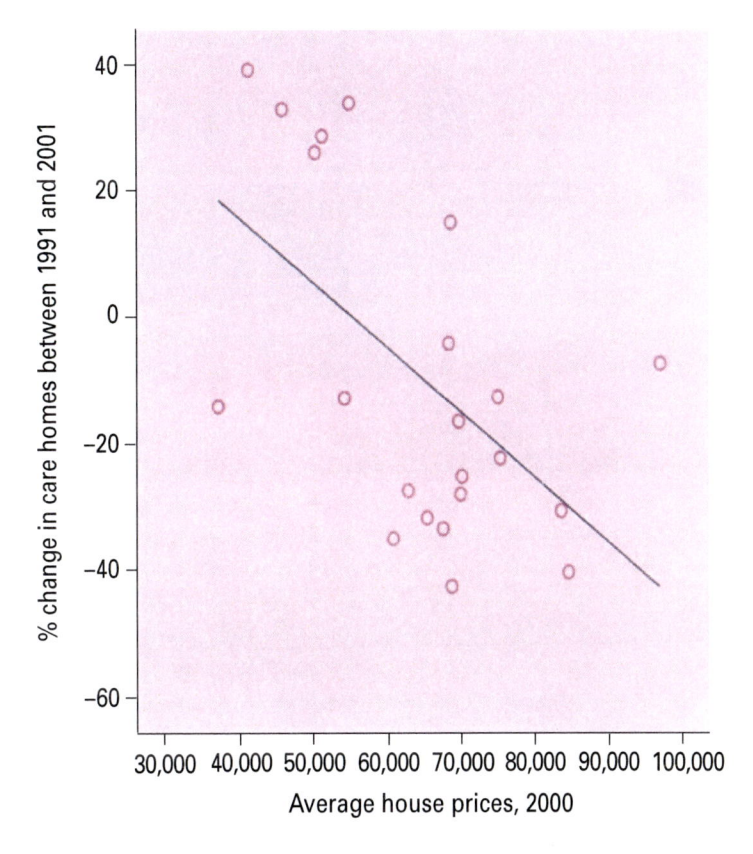

Sources: Land Registry, Census Tables ST126, ST232, KS02.
Note: $p<0.007$. R Squared Linear = 0.314.

Table 11 compares average property prices between local authority areas identified as 'exporters' and 'others'. It shows that exporting local authority areas had higher average property prices and (in 2001) still had higher percentages of their local care home stock provided directly by local government. This illustrates the difficulty with promoting market-based care home provision in these areas.

Table 11 Local authorities that are substantial exporters of supported care home residents compared with other areas

	Others	Exporters
Average property prices, Sept. 2000	£101,069	£146,568
Local authority owned care homes as a percentage of the total local stock of care homes, 2001	12%	21%

Sources: Land Registry/Census Table UV70.
Note: this cluster analysis used supported resident data for the 65+ group only.

Conclusion

In conclusion, this chapter has indicated that there are some important differences in the supply of care homes when local authorities are compared. In particular, some local authorities export a surplus of public supported residents to other places. There is no substantive evidence that the provision of public funded care home places is located in the areas where it is most needed. In the next chapter we explore the relationship of gender and marital status on the care home population.

4 Gender and marital status

Key findings

- There was a greater decline in the number of female than male care home residents, which is in part related to the slower decline of the younger section of the care home population (which comprised a greater proportion of male than female residents).

- A large majority of care home residents were female. In 2001, 63 per cent of care home residents were women aged 75 and over.

- The younger section of the care home population (under 65) was predominately male.

- In both 1991 and 2001, a woman aged 65 or over would have been more likely to be living in a care home than a man in the same age group.

- In both 1991 and 2001, for all age groups, an unmarried person (whether single, divorced or widowed) would have been more likely to be living in a care home than a married person.

- In both 1991 and 2001, a married woman in any of the older age groups (75+) would have been more likely to be living in a care home than a married man in the same age group.

- In both 1991 and 2001, an unmarried woman (single, divorced or widowed) in any of the older age groups (75+) would have been more likely to be living in a care home than an unmarried man in the same age group (except for the 75–80 age group).

- Demographic factors did not fully explain the much larger proportion of women in care homes.

- Patterns of informal caring may have had some influence on the gender imbalance in care homes, but 2001 census data did not suggest that in the older age group (75+), husbands were less likely to provide care than wives.

Changes in communal provision for adult social care 1991–2001

Gender and residential care by age groups

As shown in Figure 26, the decline in the number of care home residents disproportionately affected women. In Great Britain as a whole, the decline in the female care home population was, at 13 per cent, nearly twice the rate of the proportionate decline in the number of male care home residents, with a fall of only 7 per cent between 1991 and 2001. These differential rates of decline are, however, related to the slower rate of decline in the younger section of the care home population. This is because there were significant differences between the age distributions in the male and female care home populations, with men comprising the majority of the under-65 care home population, but only a small minority of the older population (in both 1991 and 2001). Therefore, the overall ratio of men to women in the care home population remained quite small (around 1:4).

In order to identify which gender/age groups were under- or over-represented, it was necessary to compare the proportion of care home residents in each gender and age group with the corresponding proportions in the total population. Table 12 presents the proportion of both the care home and the total population by gender for each age group. It shows that, in both census years, the majority in each age group of the total population were female, but that this proportion was much increased for the older age group (80+). Nevertheless, there was a much smaller proportion of men in the older age groups living in care homes than in the total population (of the total 75 and over population in Great Britain, men comprised 34 per cent in 1991 and 37 per cent in 2001, while only constituting 20 per cent in 1991 and 21 per cent in 2001, of the 75+ care home population).[1] However, the proportion of under 65's who were male in care homes was larger than the proportion of under 65's who were male in the total population. Therefore, older men were under-represented in care homes for both years, but the reverse was true for the younger age groups.[2] The under-representation of older men (80+) in care homes is further highlighted in Table 13. This, however, shows how this was more marked in 1991 than in 2001 (as the proportion of women in care homes fell more sharply for women than that of men between the two census years).

Gender and marital status

Figure 26 Percentage change in residents by gender and region, 1991–2001

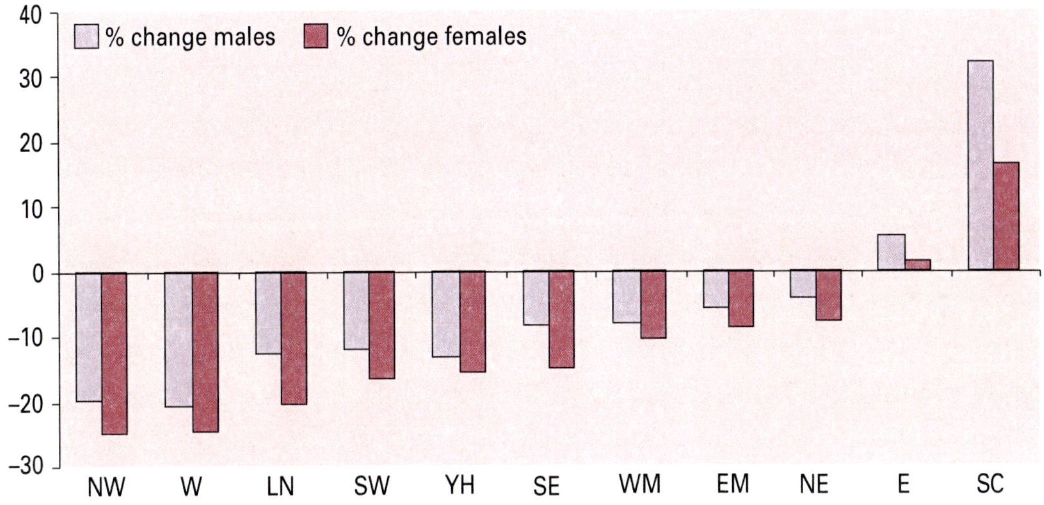

Sources: Census Tables SAS03, ST126, ST232.

Table 12 Percentage male/female in each age group of the care home population and the total population 1991–2001

Age group	Men				Women			
	Care homes		Total population		Care homes		Total population	
	1991	2001	1991	2001	1991	2001	1991	2001
16–44	59.9	58.5	49.9	49.5	40.1	41.5	50.1	50.5
45–64	53.1	56.2	49.4	49.5	46.9	43.8	50.6	50.5
65–79	35.9	37.7	43.1	45.0	64.1	62.3	56.9	55.0
80+	18.0	19.1	29.7	34.1	82.0	80.9	70.3	65.9

Source: Sample of Anonymised Records 1991/2001.

Table 13 Percentage of the total population that live in care homes by gender and age group 1991–2001

Age group	Men		Women	
	1991	2001	1991	2001
16–64	0.13	0.13	0.09	0.10
65–74	0.9	0.7	1.0	0.7
75–79	2.3	1.8	3.3	2.6
80–84	5.5	3.3	9.2	6.0
85–89	10.5	8.4	19.2	13.7
90+	22.6	16.3	33.4	28.5

Source: Sample of Anonymised Records 1991/2001.

Changes in communal provision for adult social care 1991–2001

Marital status and residential care by age groups

In terms of marital status, the most prominent difference between the care home population and the total population was the much higher proportion of widowed people in the care home population (61 per cent in 2001). This is of course in part because of the older age distribution in care homes than in the general population. The following Tables 14 (1991) and 15 (2001), therefore, show the proportions by marital status and age group for both the care home population and the total population. These show that (both in 1991 and 2001), for each age group, care homes comprised a larger proportion of widowed and single people and a smaller proportion of married people than the total population.

It should be noted that, as shown in the tables, the 2001 SAR has an additional category of 'separated'. This refers to persons who are separated but still legally married.

Table 14 Distribution of the care home/total population by marital status 1991 (per cent)

Marital status	16–74 Care homes	16–74 Total population	75–84 Care homes	75–84 Total population	85+ Care homes	85+ Total population
Single	59.5	28.8	18.0	8.5	16.3	11.8
Married	9.6	52.9	10.9	36.3	5.4	14.7
Remarried	1.3	7.0	1.2	5.3	0.8	2.8
Divorced	7.1	6.4	2.0	2.0	0.8	1.1
Widowed	22.5	5.0	68.0	47.9	76.6	69.5
Total	100	100	100	100	100	100

Source: Sample of Anonymised Records 1991.

Table 15 Distribution of the care home/total population by marital status 2001 (per cent)

Marital status	16–74 Care homes	16–74 Total population	75–84 Care homes	75–84 Total population	85+ Care homes	85+ Total population
Single	61.8	33.2	16.4	6.7	12.0	8.2
Married	10.1	44.3	13.4	39.9	6.4	18.6
Remarried	1.3	7.3	0.8	5.6	0.7	3.5
Separated	1.8	2.6	0.6	0.6	0.2	0.3
Divorced	9.5	8.6	3.2	3.5	1.1	1.9
Widowed	15.6	3.9	65.5	43.7	79.7	67.5
Total	100	100	100	100	100	100

Source: Sample of Anonymised Records 2001.

The relationship between marital status, gender and age

As described above, women are more likely to be living in care homes than men and single people are more likely to live in care homes than the married. As shown in Figure 27, however, this is not purely owing to demographic factors, such as the greater longevity of women or the high proportion of widowed people (mostly female) in the older age group. The greater likelihood of single people (than married) and women (than men) living in a care home applies for each of the older age groups (except for the 75–79 age group in which there was a slightly larger proportion of unmarried men than unmarried women living in residential care). Thus, for example, even if a person was in the oldest age group (90+) and married, the chances of living in a care home would be increased if the person were female rather than male. Within each age group, however, an unmarried man would be more likely to live in a care home than a married woman.

Figure 27 Percentage of people living in care homes by gender, age and marital status

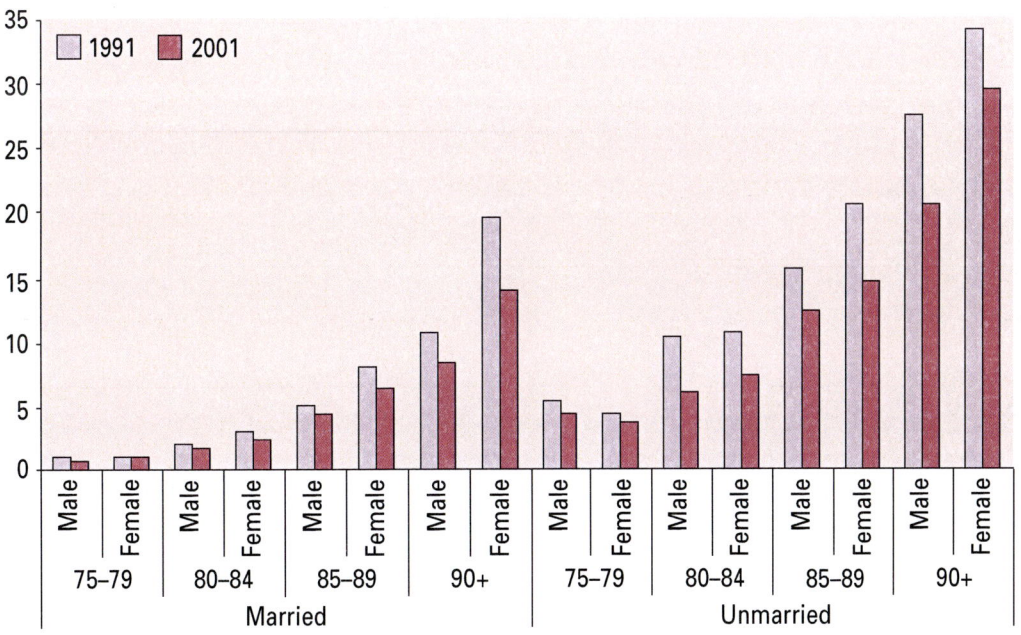

Source: Sample of Anonymised Records 1991–2001.
Notes: 'married' combines categories: 'married', 'remarried' and 'separated'; 'unmarried' combines categories: 'single', 'widowed' and 'divorced'.

Changes in communal provision for adult social care 1991–2001

The particular significance of marital status as a determining factor is highlighted in Table 16, which shows a combined probability model. This model enabled a more precise examination of the combined influence of the three factors, on the probability of living in a care home and then to see how this changed from 1991 to 2001. It shows, for example, that unmarried people (which includes widows, divorced and single) were 4.428 times more likely to be living in care homes than married people, when controlling for the influence of gender and age (if just the odds of being single were computed, without controlling for the influence of gender and age, the odds would be much higher).

When the odds of women being resident in a care home were computed as a single event, women were more than twice as likely as men to be living in a care home. However, even when the other demographic factors were controlled (age and marital status), the conclusion of the combined model is that women were still marginally more likely than men (odds greater than one) to be in care homes. The odds of gender influencing the combined situation marginally increased in 2001.

As it has been established that other factors beyond those of a basic demographic nature must have been of influence on the under-representation of men in care homes, the question is therefore raised as to what these might be.

One possible explanatory factor may be a greater level of care available to men. Unfortunately, there is no census data available on the characteristics of people in receipt of (only on those who provide) unpaid care, so there are limitations on the extent to which this can be explored.

Table 16 Model to predict residence in care home 1991 and 2001 (UK residents aged 75 and over)

	Odds Ratio (Exp. B)
1991	
Unmarried/married	4.428
85 and over/under 85	4.257
Women/men	1.191
2001	
Unmarried/married	3.939
85 and over/under 85	4.588
Women/men	1.286

Source: Census – Sample of Anonymised Records 1991/2001.
Notes: logistic regression analysis.
All odds ratios shown are significant to p <0.005.

Gender and marital status

The data does show, however, that men in the older age group (75+) are no less likely to provide unpaid care than women in the same age group. In fact, for Great Britain as a whole in 2001, the proportion of men who provide care (11.3 per cent) is almost twice the proportion of women providing care in the same age group (6.1 per cent). This is related, though, to the fact that married people are much more likely to provide care and that men are much more likely than women to be married (as a greater proportion of women are widowed). Nevertheless, even if we take only married people in this age group, results show that women were still no more likely to provide care. In fact, the 2001 SAR shows that, in the 75+ age group, almost exactly the same proportion of married women (15.6 per cent) provided care as did married men (15.7 per cent). Women were, however, slightly more likely to provide 'intensive' (i.e. 20+ hours) of care (10.2 per cent) than men (9.6 per cent) in the older (75+) age group. However, this data does not suggest that there is any significant relationship between the larger proportion of married women (than married men) in care homes and a lack of informal care provided by husbands (in relation to the amount of care provided by wives in the same age group).

However, it should be noted that data on informal caring is of course self-reported, and therefore it is possible, for example, that men may have been more likely to identify themselves as care providers than women involved in carrying out the same caring tasks. Another problem is that, as no data was available on who care is provided *for*, we cannot ascertain whether, for example, other carers such as offspring or other relatives may have been more likely to provide care for a male (rather than female) relative. Thus, census data is limited in its usefulness for exploring the question as to why older women are more likely to enter care homes than older men, especially in regard to any influence there may be in the availability of informal care. Further research is needed in order to explore this issue in more depth.

Conclusion

In conclusion, this chapter has shown the gender imbalance in the care home population, with two-thirds of them being women aged 75 and over. Having a surviving marital partner seems to increase one's chances of avoiding residence in a care home. Although married women often outlive male partners, this factor alone does not explain fully the large number of women in the care home population. In the next chapter we review the extent to which the minority ethnic population is represented in the care home population.

5 Ethnicity

It should be noted that the classifications used in this chapter are based on secondary census definitions that the researchers had no ability to change. Even when using full census data for the UK, there are also methodological challenges in that the sub-sample of older people from ethnic minorities is small. For the purpose of most of our analysis we have therefore found it necessary to combine census groups into two categories: 'white' and 'minority ethnic'. 'White' includes white minority ethnic groups (e.g. Irish) as well as 'white British'. All other ethnic groups are included within the term 'minority ethnic'. We are aware that this will mask differences between the various ethnic groups. In a few parts of our analysis we have attempted to use the census sub-categories of Asian and black. This was to try and obtain a more accurate analysis of the impact on ethnic minorities where sufficient data was judged to be available. However, when using the census SAR, the sub-samples of older people in ethnic minorities are in some cases too small to achieve significant results without combining groups. Even when combined, however, it should be noted that the numbers in the 85+ minority ethnic group are still very small, and these results should therefore be treated with caution.[1]

Key findings

- In 1991 and 2001, census data shows that the proportion of the minority ethnic population living in care homes was smaller than the proportion of the white population living in care homes. This was the case for the younger as well as for the older age groups.

- Data from the 2001 SAR suggests that the Asian/Asian British population were the most under-represented in care homes. This was the case for both the 75+ and the 16–74 age groups.

- A large proportion of minority ethnic people live in London, where a lower than average proportion of people live in care homes. However, this alone does not explain the national under-representation of people from ethnic minorities in care homes.

- In 2001, the minority ethnic care home population was relatively less well represented in London (for both the younger and the older age group) in comparison with the white population.

- Data suggests that the large decline of care home residents in London between 1991 and 2001 particularly impacted on the minority ethnic population.

- In 2001, the minority ethnic older (75+) population was less well represented (than the older white population) in care homes in all regions of Great Britain except the North East.

- In 2001, in most regions of Britain, the under 75 minority ethnic population was less well represented in care homes than the corresponding white population. This was, however, not the case in the East Midlands, East, South West and Wales.

- Data on unpaid care is lacking, but data available for 2001 suggests that minority ethnic older people were less likely to live alone and were more likely to live in a household with someone who identified themselves as an unpaid carer. This seems to have particularly been the case for the Asian/Asian British community than for the other categories included in the 'minority ethnic' group.

Ethnicity and residential care by age groups

If the care home population is compared with the total population, the minority ethnic group appears to be less well represented in care homes in comparison with the white group. However, any comparison of the ethnic make-up of the two populations must take into account the differential age distributions. Is the apparent under-representation of the minority ethnic group simply a result of the younger age profile in comparison with the white population? In order to address this question, it is necessary to look at the proportion of people living in care homes by ethnicity and age group.

Table 17 shows that the percentage of people living in care homes declined for all age groups in both the minority ethnic and the white group, but this appears to have had slightly more impact on the former. Also it is evident that, for both years, there was a higher proportion of the white group living in care homes than minority ethnic people for each of the three age groups. This suggests that those in the minority ethnic group in both the younger and the older age groups were less well represented in care homes in Great Britain.

Changes in communal provision for adult social care 1991–2001

Table 17 Percentage of white/minority ethnic persons living in care homes by age group

Age group	White 1991	White 2001	Minority ethnic 1991	Minority ethnic 2001
16–74	0.29	0.25	0.23	0.13
75–84	5.0	4.0	3.9	2.6
85+	21.6	19.5	14.9	9.6

Source: Sample of Anonymised Records 1991/2001.

Although, as noted above, this data should be viewed with caution, 2001 SARs data for England and Wales suggests that the low proportion of the minority ethnic population living in care homes may be most evident among the Asian/Asian British community. Only 2.8 per cent of people aged 75+ in the Asian/Asian British[2] group were living in care homes in comparison with 7.9 per cent for the white population of the same age group, 6.0 per cent for the mixed and 4.0 per cent for other minority ethnic groups.[3] Findings from the 2001 SAR also showed the Asian/Asian British group to have the smallest proportion of adults under 75 living in care homes (0.07 per cent compared with 0.30 for whites, 0.20 for the mixed group and 0.19 for black and all other minority ethnic categories).

Ethnicity and residential care by area

Location is an important factor when looking at ethnicity, because minority ethnic communities are concentrated in particular parts of the UK. Although the mean proportion of people in a local authority area who were from a minority ethnic group was 8.4 per cent in 2001, the median was 2.8 per cent, with the majority (51 per cent) consisting of less than 3 per cent persons who identified as belonging to any ethnic group other than white.

As shown in Figure 28, people classed as belonging to a minority ethnic group are much more likely to live in urban areas, where (as discussed in Chapter 3) there tends to be a lower proportion of people living in care homes. This is particularly true of London, which has the highest minority ethnic population. In fact, 2001 figures show that nearly half the total UK minority ethnic population (45 per cent) lives in London.[4] It is therefore necessary to consider the relationship between the apparent under-representation of people from ethnic minorities and location. Is this under-representation simply because of the tendency to live in areas (especially London) that have a low proportion of people of all ethnic groups in care homes, or are people from ethnic minorities still comparatively less well represented in these communities when compared with the majority ethnic population in the same communities?

Ethnicity

Table 18 shows that in 1991 for both the older and younger age groups there was very little difference between the proportions of white/minority ethnic persons living in care homes, but that in 2001 the minority ethnic group appeared to be less well represented. This suggests that the under-representation of minority ethnic people in Great Britain living in residential and nursing care was not simply because such a large proportion of the minority ethnic population were living in London (at least in 2001). It also suggests that the decline of nursing and residential care in London has affected the minority ethnic group to a greater extent than the white group both in Inner and Outer London.

Figure 28 Scatterplot showing the relationship between the percentage of people aged 75+ living in care homes and the percentage of the 75+ total population who are from a minority ethnic group, 2001, by local authority area

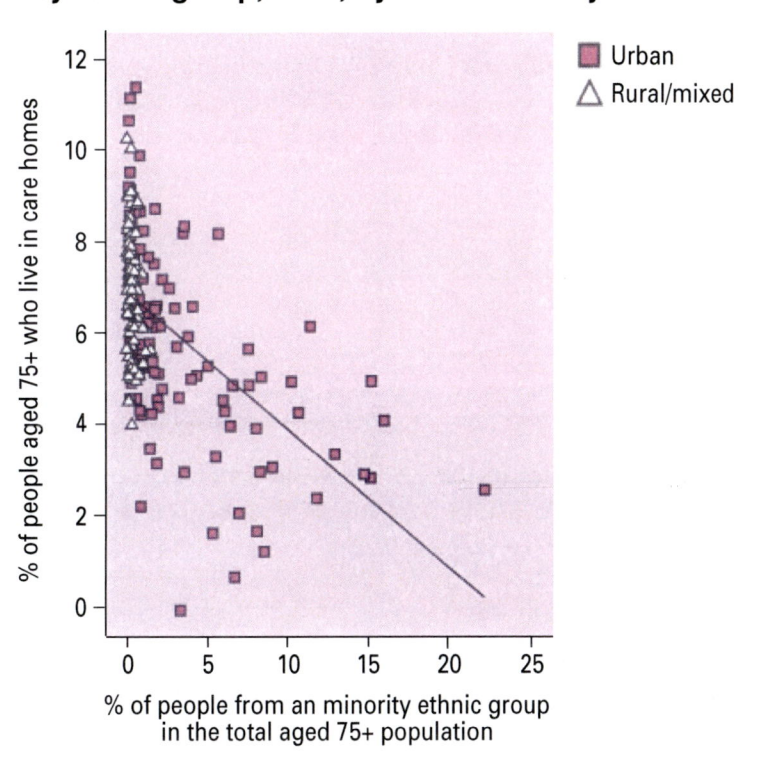

Source: Census Tables KS02, ST126, ST232, ST101, ST201.
Notes: sig. (two tailed) = <0.0005. R Squared Linear = 0.294.

Table 18 Percentage living in care homes in London by ethnicity and age group

Age group	White		Minority ethnic	
	1991	2001	1991	2001
16–74				
Inner London	0.24	0.12	0.26	0.06
Outer London	0.19	0.22	0.21	0.10
75 and over				
Inner London	5.3	3.0	5.4	2.0
Outer London	5.4	5.4	5.0	4.5

Source: Sample of Anonymised Records 1991/2001.

Changes in communal provision for adult social care 1991–2001

Figure 29 supports the hypothesis that the low proportion of the minority ethnic group in care homes is not simply the result of the concentration of ethnic minorities in particular areas of the country. In fact, the figure illustrates that, in each region (except for the North East), the proportion of older (75+) minority ethnic people in care homes is smaller than the proportion of people from the minority ethnic category in the total population (for the same age group). Figure 30 shows that the minority ethnic group was also more poorly represented in the younger section of the care home population in most regions (but not in the East Midlands, East, South West and Wales).[5]

Figure 29 Percentage of the 75+ care home/total population who are from a minority ethnic group, 2001, by region

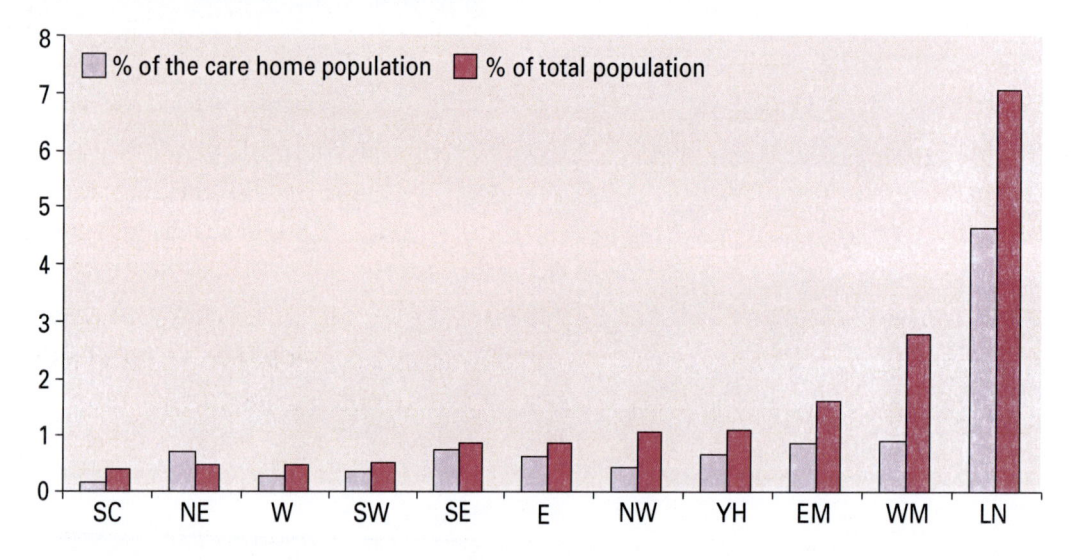

Sources: Census Tables M242, ST125, ST228.

Figure 30 Percentage of the 16–74 care home/total population who are from a minority ethnic group, 2001, by region

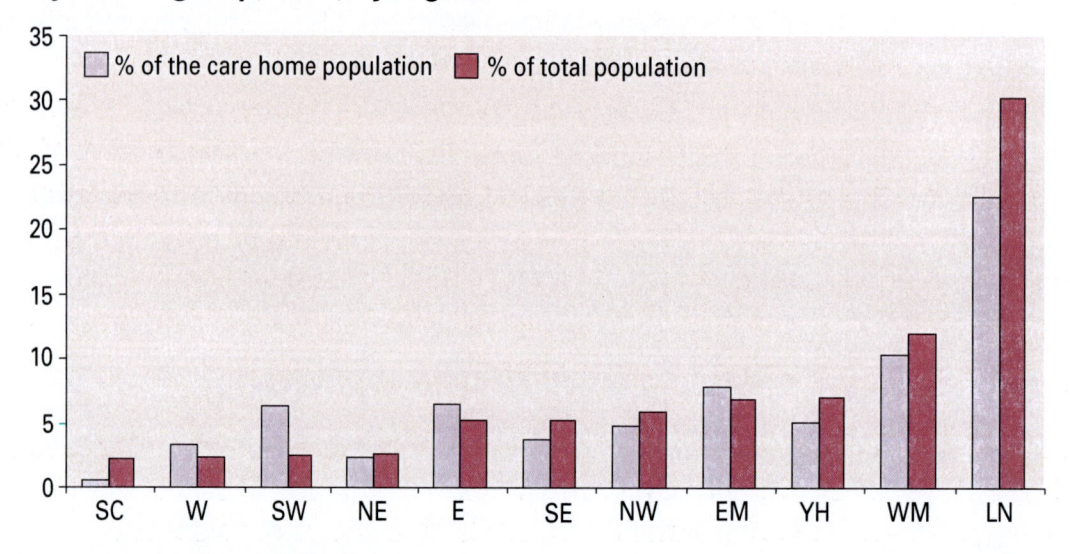

Sources: Census Tables M242, ST125, ST228.

Ethnicity and informal care

We were interested in whether there was a relationship between any differential levels of informal care in white/minority ethnic communities and the differences in the proportions living in care homes. Census data available on this topic was, however, insufficient to be able to ascertain whether minority ethnic people are more likely to receive unpaid care than white people.[6]

The data that is available can give only a vague indication of the situation with regard to ethnicity and family care patterns. The 2001 SAR shows that the proportion of people in the minority ethnic group providing unpaid care was smaller (7.8 per cent or 1:13) than the proportion of white people providing unpaid care (10.3 per cent or 1:10). However, the differential age distributions of both sections of the population should be taken into account. Census tables show that although the overall population was over 8 per cent minority ethnic, less than 2 per cent of the 75+ population were from a minority ethnic group (in 2001). Thus the white population has a much 'older' age profile, than the minority ethnic population. According to data from the 2001 SAR, the ratio of older (75+) to younger persons in the minority ethnic group was 1:47, which compares to 1:11 for the total population. In this demographic context, the lesser likelihood of minority ethnic persons providing care is unlikely to equate to a smaller proportion of minority ethnic elders being cared for.

Other data in fact suggests that older persons in the minority ethnic group may be more likely to be in receipt of informal care.[7] As shown in the following chapter, in London the proportion of households with one person aged 75+ with a limiting long-term illness who has a carer living in the household is relatively high. Within London, as shown in Figure 31, there was a positive association between this unpaid care variable and the proportion of persons of an ethnic minority in an area. This, however, was only statistically significant in Outer London[8], which suggests this may have been influenced by the different ethnic compositions of Outer and Inner London. In particular, it is notable that the Pakistani and Indian groups made up a much larger proportion of the population of Outer London than Inner London.[9] If the minority ethnic population (excluding mixed) is divided into Asian and black, the association was much stronger for the Asian group.[10] It should also be noted that there was not a significant association between this unpaid care variable and deprivation indices,[11] which suggests that ethnicity is a more significant factor in determining levels of unpaid care than deprivation.

Another indication that older persons in the minority ethnic group may have been more likely to receive care from family members is the greater likelihood that a person aged 75+ has of living with others. SARs data shows considerable

Changes in communal provision for adult social care 1991–2001

differences between the two groups in England and Wales,[12] with nearly half (48 per cent) of white older persons living alone and 92 per cent living either alone or with one other person, compared with only 31 per cent living alone and 59 per cent either alone or with one other person in the minority ethnic sample. Perhaps more surprisingly, as many as 12 per cent of the minority ethnic group live in a household with six or more residents, compared with just 0.4 per cent in the white group. As shown in Figure 32, this data also shows that, although older people in the black/ black British group were slightly more likely to live in larger family structures than the white group, the significant differences are evident for the Asian/Asian British group.[13] Also, the 2001 SAR shows that among people in the sample aged 75+ (living in households), white (20 per cent) were less likely than minority ethnic (32 per cent) older people to have one or more unpaid carers living in the same household. Again, the Asian/Asian British group is particularly notable. When the data is compared for the five ethnic categories available in the SAR, older people from this ethnic group are shown to have been by far the most likely to have an unpaid carer living in the same household (42 per cent). It is therefore likely that higher rates of informal caring may be an important factor in accounting for the comparatively low proportion of older Asian/Asian British people living in care homes.

Figure 31 Scatterplot showing the relationship between the proportion of households with one person aged 75+ with an LLTI where there is also a carer, and the proportion of the population from a minority ethnic group, 2001, by London local authority area

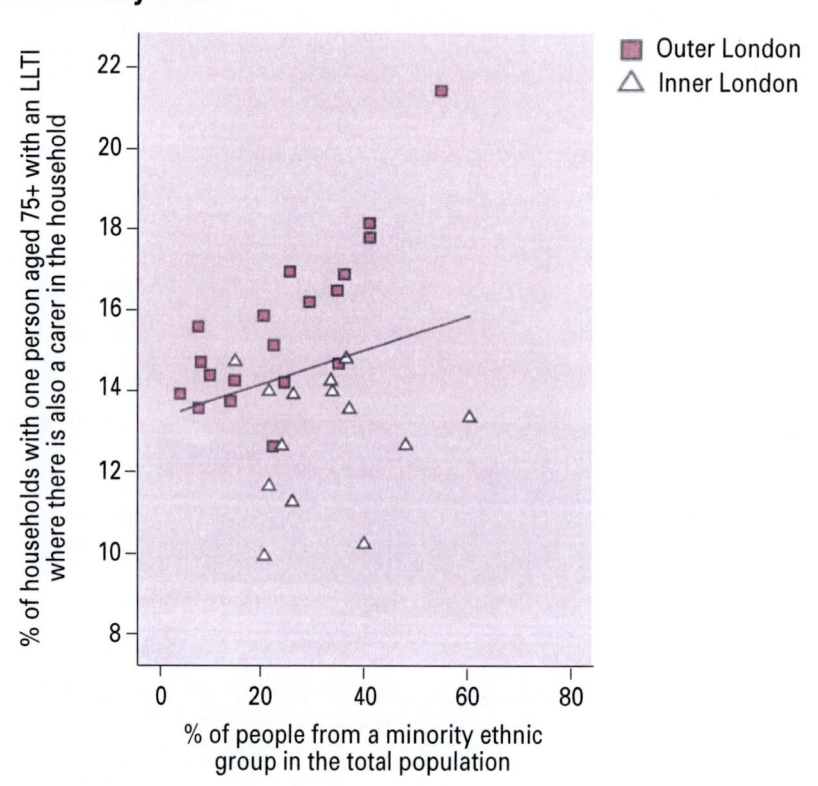

Sources: Census Tables ST027, ST101, ST201.
R Squared Linear = 0.064.

Ethnicity

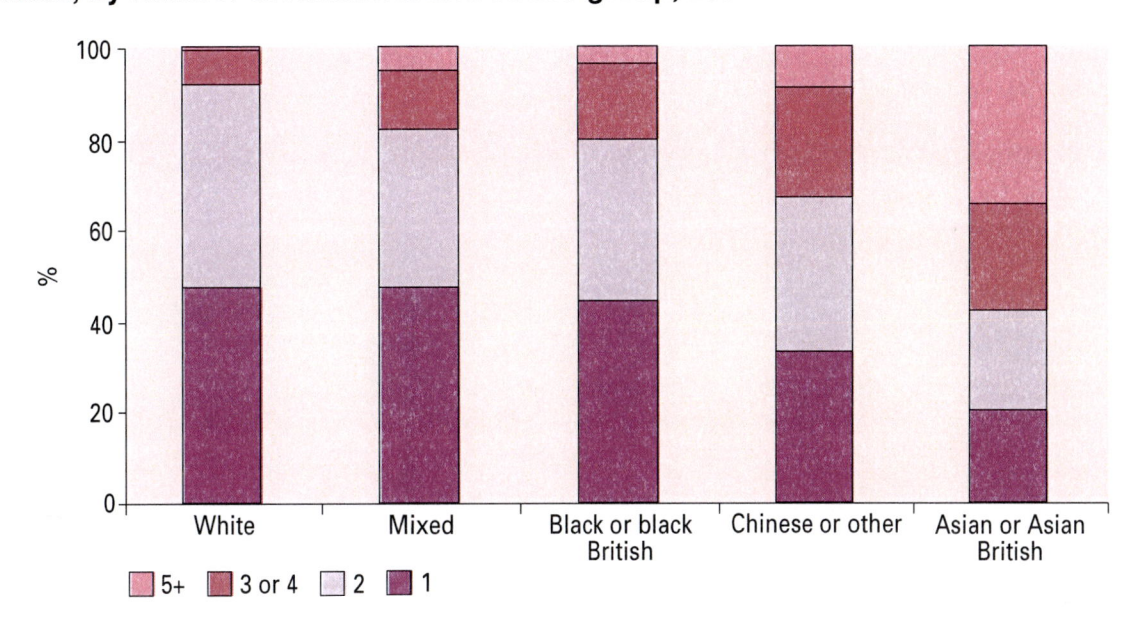

Figure 32 Proportion of people aged 75+ living in households in England and Wales, by number of residents and ethnic group, 2001

Source: Sample of Anonymised Records, 2001.

Conclusion

In conclusion, this chapter has shown that the proportion of the minority ethnic population living in care homes was smaller that the proportion of the white population living in care homes. It would seem that the decline of care home residents in London between 1991 and 2001 had a particular impact on the large minority ethnic population in London. In the next chapter we examine the relationship between residential care and other types of home-based social care.

6 Relationship between residential care and other types of care

This chapter looks at the changing relationship between local authority supported residential care and other types of care in the 1990s.

Key findings

- There is no uniform association between local authorities experiencing a greater decline in residential care provision and a growth of home care services.

- Of the three countries, there was a substantially lower proportion of older people providing informal care in Scotland, while Wales had the highest proportion.

- No relationship was identified between changes in household structure and changes in residential care provision.

- There was a decline in older people living in other medical/care establishments in all regions but this was particularly substantial in Scotland, which may be one reason for the increase in residential and nursing care in Scotland.

Home care services

Given the policy change after the 1990 NHS and Community Care Act with the attempt to increase community care and home care services, set against the gradual reduction of residential care in many places during the next decade, we might expect to find that local authorities with higher levels of supported home care services had achieved this against comparably lower levels of supported residential care. Previous research has suggested that, post 1991, some substitution of residential care for home care did begin to take place (Knapp *et al.*, 2001). But Figure 33 shows a positive association among England's local authorities between the amounts of supported home care for older people and supported residential care in 2001 ($r=0.440$, $p<0.0005$, $N=149$). This means that there is a tendency for local authorities that provide high levels of residential care to provide relatively high levels of home care services too. We also examined this relationship for earlier years and found a very similar pattern. This fits with national data that shows how government

Relationship between residential care and other types of care

expenditure on residential care continued to rise steadily throughout the decade, before reaching a plateau in 2001–02 (Department of Health, 2004). Although government expenditure on home care services also increased in the same decade,[1] this was not achieved by a reduction in expenditure on residential care.

This data suggests that the substitution of residential care with home care has not been achieved on a large scale, but rather varies from place to place. The association between home and residential care provision is particularly weak in London (r = 0.302) and not significant. There is also some marked variation among the inner-city boroughs that export numerous supported residents to other areas. One of the largest exporters, Camden, had (in 2001) similar levels of supported funding for older people in residential care to several other London boroughs, but a much higher number of older people over 65 helped to live at home. Again, this suggests the importance of examining change on a local case study basis, in particular when looking at the ability of local authorities to move resources into community-based home care services.

Figure 33 The relationship between local authority supported home care and care supported in residential homes by English local authority, 2001

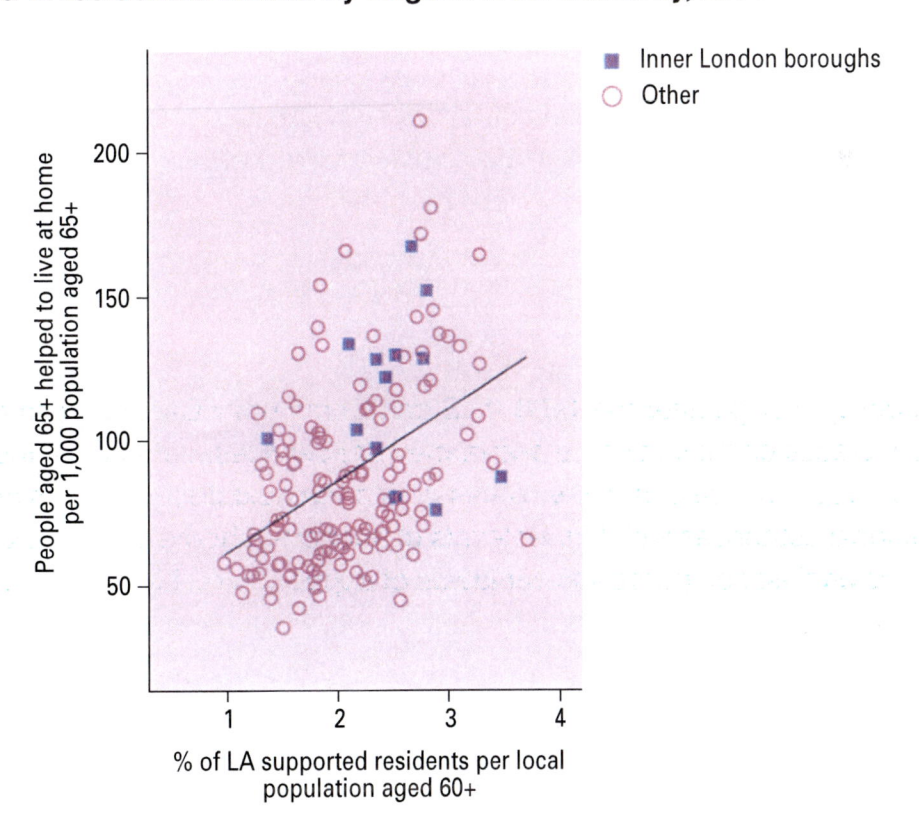

Source: Department of Health, KIGS dataset, 2003.
Notes: p = 0.029. R Squared Linear = 0.194.

Changes in communal provision for adult social care 1991–2001

Unpaid care

Data is available for 2001 on the number of people who reported providing unpaid care.[2] There are a number of limitations with this data that make it difficult to assess whether there was any relationship between levels of unpaid care and the proportion of people living in care homes. The main obstacle is the lack of data available on *receivers* of unpaid care. It is therefore, for example, not possible to explore a straightforward association between the number of older people receiving unpaid care and the number of older people living in care homes in an area.

The proportion of people providing unpaid care may give some indication, but results are skewed by the likelihood that, in areas with higher numbers of older people, there would have been more people providing unpaid care. The proportion of older people providing care was therefore felt to give a better indication of the comparative prevalence of unpaid care in an area. Interestingly, these results show that there is a substantial difference between the proportion of older people (75+) providing care in Scotland (6.0 per cent) when compared with England (8.1 per cent) and Wales (8.7 per cent). The proportion of both men and women in this age group reporting to provide care was smaller in Scotland.[3] The methodological problem of the self-reported nature of this variable should, however, be emphasised.

There is also a census variable available on households containing one person aged 75+ with a limiting long-term illness, which also contained a person identifying him/herself as a provider of care. We therefore have two pieces of information, i.e. that there is a carer in the household and that there is a person likely to be in need of care in the same household, but we have no way of knowing whether the two were linked. It could have been in some cases, for example, that the carer was caring for someone living elsewhere, or perhaps for a younger person with a disability who was living in the same household. It could also be in some cases that the person with the LLTI is also the carer, i.e. s/he is caring for a friend or family member living elsewhere. Nevertheless, if it is supposed that in the majority of cases the two are connected, data (as shown in Figure 34) suggests that there may be an association between higher levels of unpaid care and a lower proportion living in care homes. However, the association between the proportion of people aged 75+ with a limiting long-term illness who also have a carer living with them in the household[4] is very weak and statistically significant only if the South West is removed (the scatterplot shows the South West to have the highest level both of unpaid care and of residential care).

Figure 34 Scatterplot showing the relationship between the proportion of households with one person aged 75+ with an LLTI where there is also a carer, and the proportion of the older (75+) population living in care homes by region, 2001

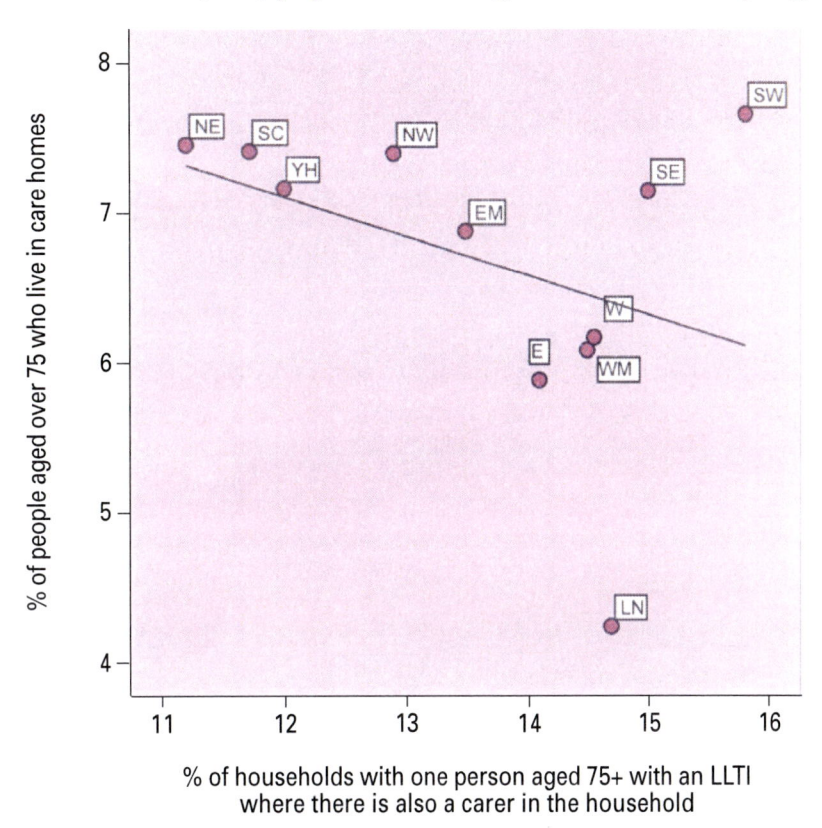

[Scatterplot with x-axis "% of households with one person aged 75+ with an LLTI where there is also a carer in the household" ranging 11-16, and y-axis "% of people aged over 75 who live in care homes" ranging 4-8. Data points labelled: NE, SC, YH, NW, EM, SE, SW, E, W, WM, LN.]

Sources: Census Tables ST027, ST126, ST232.
Notes: sig. (two tailed) = 0.245 (without South West = 0.043). R Squared Linear = 0.147.

Household structure

One problem with the data displayed in Figure 34 is that it does not give any indication of the level of unpaid care received by older persons in lone-person households, in which 44 per cent of persons aged 75+ were living (both in 1991 and 2001, having declined very slightly by just 0.2 per cent during the decade).[5] It is probable, though, that this group would have been the least likely to receive unpaid care because of the absence of a spouse (and for the 'never married' group the decreased likelihood of having offspring).

No association was found, however, between the proportion of older persons living alone and the proportion living in care homes by region, in 1991 ($r = -0.417$, $p = 0.202$) or in 2001 ($r = -0.232$, $p = 0.493$). In both years, London in particular contradicts the hypothesis that there should be more residential care in areas with a higher proportion of older people living alone. London, in fact, had a high proportion of older people living alone, while having the lowest proportion living in care homes.

Changes in communal provision for adult social care 1991–2001

The South West also stood out from the expected pattern, having, in both years, the lowest proportion living alone (for the 75+ age group) while having the highest proportion in care homes. There was also no association at a regional or local authority level between the percentage change in people aged 75+ living in lone-person households and the percentage change in those living in care homes in the same age group ($r = -0.036$, $p = 0.612$).

Table 19 does not highlight any particular relationship between changing household structures by region and changes in the proportions living in care homes. It shows in fact that there was overall, and in most regions, a percentage increase in both lone-person and two+-person households in the 75+ age group, while the proportion of those living in care homes and other medical/care establishments declined. The comparatively large decline in the proportion of older people living in other medical/care establishments in Scotland should, however, be noted. Those in the 75+ age group living in other medical/care establishments in Scotland declined by 7,469 (from 12,405 in 1991 to 4,936 in 2001), while those living in care homes increased by 4,412 (from 22,132 in 1991 to 26,544 in 2001). This may therefore be an explanatory factor for the increase in residential and nursing care in Scotland. It should also be noted that London had the highest proportion of people aged 75+ living in other medical/care establishments.

Table 19 Living arrangements of people aged 75 and over by region, 1991/2001 (per cent)

Region	Care homes 1991	Care homes 2001	Other medical/care establishments 1991	Other medical/care establishments 2001	In household (alone) 1991	In household (alone) 2001	In household (2+/other*) 1991	In household (2+/other*) 2001
North East	9.0	7.4	1.4	0.4	47.0	46.5	42.6	45.6
North West	10.0	7.4	0.8	0.4	44.4	45.3	44.7	47.0
Yorks and Humber	9.2	7.2	0.7	0.5	46.0	45.0	44.2	47.3
East Midlands	8.9	6.9	0.6	0.4	43.4	43.0	47.1	49.8
West Midlands	7.8	6.1	0.8	0.4	43.4	43.5	48.0	50.0
East	6.8	5.9	1.1	0.4	42.6	43.0	49.5	50.6
London	5.1	4.3	1.1	0.7	46.3	46.9	47.6	48.1
South East	8.9	7.1	1.2	0.4	40.9	42.4	48.9	50.0
South West	10.3	7.6	0.8	0.4	39.0	40.9	49.9	51.1
Scotland	6.8	7.4	3.8	1.4	45.8	46.3	43.6	45.0
Wales	8.7	6.2	1.0	0.6	41.2	43.0	49.1	50.2
England	8.4	6.6	0.9	0.4	43.3	43.8	47.3	49.1
Great Britain	8.3	6.7	1.2	0.5	43.4	44.0	47.1	48.8

Sources: Census Tables SAS02, LBS04, SAS47, KS02, ST126, ST232, TT006, TT020.
* 'Other' refers to the small number living in non-medical/care establishments.

Conclusion

To conclude, census data does not suggest that there is any overall strong relationship between the availability of unpaid care and the distribution of residential/nursing care. However, further qualitative research is required in order to explore decision-making processes in relation to individuals' care needs and how these are influenced by or impact on the level and nature of local care provision.

7 Conclusions

The data in this report confirms that some decline in care home provision between 1991 and 2001 in many regions and areas of Britain was as expected, given the policy objective of the 1990 NHS and Community Care Act. The Act sought to encourage a much greater diversity of community care provision and to end the growth of residential social care. There were also policy and social trends working against a sharper decline in care homes during this decade.

First, the total size and proportion of the older population, particularly the over 85s, was growing. Second, hospital care was becoming increasingly focused on short-term admissions for medical treatment, with continuing attempts to reduce length of stay in the acute hospital environment. Given these two factors, it is clear why care home provision did not decline more rapidly (although Department of Health data since 2001 suggests it has continued to decline in England). Funding for residential care continued to take a large proportion of government expenditure on social care between 1991 and 2001.

Some policy commentators are concerned about the care home population declining at all, given the rising older population and changing focus of the NHS. Such commentators imply that central government and local government should seek to estimate the national/regional/local level of care homes that are needed and then ensure they are provided (Coms-Herrera *et al.*, 2001).

Such planning could aim to prevent decline occurring too rapidly in certain localities and to ensure that a reasonable equity exists between regions. The provision of nursing and residential care is still a central element of the health and social care approach in modern Britain and an equitable distribution by region is important. Our findings suggest that the regional distribution of care homes has become more equitable between 1991 and 2001.

The recent Government Green Paper, *Independence, Well-being and Choice* (Department of Health, 2005), has provided a vision of a new social care market that is driven by individual user power and choice, rather than provider interests and state purchasing power. If implemented, this will provide a further dimension to the development of the social care market. It will not necessarily challenge the need for a care home sector. Demand for a 'care bridge' between the NHS and independence at home will always remain, given the pressures of demand for health care and the need to minimise the time patients spend in hospital. Government policy will continue to need to specify how it will support and plan for the stability and quality of the care home sector alongside funding for care provided in people's homes.

Conclusions

The type of homes in decline

It is surprising to find that decline seems to affect nursing homes more than residential homes. There is reason to doubt the ability of the Census to correctly classify the type of care homes, because it does not have a classification of dual registration. But the decline that is demonstrated in nursing homes rather than residential homes is also evident in Department of Health (2001) data. Our figures show an 18 per cent decline in nursing homes between 1991 and 2001. This is the loss in Britain of 1,075 nursing homes, which is surprising given the reduction in hospital admission times and the pressure to discharge people more rapidly from hospital. One might have anticipated a need for more nursing homes, but perhaps less long-term residential care.

There is not a uniform national decline in residential care and indeed, when nursing home figures are removed from the analysis, the overall ten-year trend for Britain looks more stable, although there are important differences within countries, regions and local areas.

The most notable national trend from 1991 to 2001 for residential homes is that supply has moved away from the local authority to the independent sector. Local authority homes had declined by 54 per cent in Britain with the closure of 2,826 homes. If the average value of these local government homes was £150,000 this represents a sale of local authority assets worth £424 million. This decline in local authority homes was against a background of earlier decline in the same sector in the 1980s (House of Commons Health Committee, 1996, p. x, Table 1). In some places this decline was met by growth in the independent sector, but certainly not in all places. In fact over a quarter (28 per cent) of local authority areas in Great Britain experienced decline in the number of care homes in both sectors.

In Britain, independent residential homes (not including nursing homes) had actually increased by 13 per cent with an increase of 1,480 homes. Despite this change in the ownership and supply of care home services, many places in homes are still partly, or completely, purchased by local government on behalf of service users. This policy has become known as 'supported places'. This has created its own unintended consequences, for example, a two-tier pricing system (Office of Fair Trading, 2005). This is where private self-funding residents are charged a different rate to 'supported places' purchased by local government. Our research has shown that there is not necessarily a relationship between the supply located within a local authority area and the number of supported places purchased by that local authority. The reason for this is that, increasingly, urban local authorities look to purchase places that are located in other outside areas. This has been discussed extensively in this report as the policy of 'exporting'.

Country and regional variations

Our research found considerable variation in trends between the countries of England, Scotland and Wales. The number of care homes in Wales declined the most (–18 per cent), while there was an increase in homes in Scotland (+11 per cent). Wales is the only country in Britain where all three types of care home declined, including independent residential homes. Scotland was the only country to show a slight increase in the number of nursing care homes. It has not been possible to compare figures for Northern Ireland between 1991 and 2001, but the 2001 figures show a relatively high proportion of older people living in care homes when compared to the other countries of the UK.

Within English regions there was a narrowing in the differences, in terms of the proportion of people living in care homes. Similar to Wales, the North West of England had experienced a comparatively higher level of decline (–21 per cent) in the total number of care homes. Also, when examining regions, there was no general association between a decline in local authority care homes and an increase in independent care homes.

Overall, market provision of care homes is not uniform. It seems to be related to a complex range of factors, including, in some regions, changes in house prices and, to a limited extent, local politics. House prices seemed to have some relationship to the greater decline in the number of homes in London and Wales, but this association could not be demonstrated in other parts of Britain.

Scotland

It is important to attempt to understand why the trend in care home provision in Scotland between 1991 and 2001 is different from other regions of Britain. It would appear that the independent sector developed and grew much later in Scotland than in England. Similarly, the closing of large institutions, such as geriatric wards in hospitals, also appears to have happened later than in England and Wales. This is reflected in the statistics that we have examined for older people living in other medical and care communal establishments (that is, communal establishments other than residential and nursing care establishments), which showed a higher level in 1991 when compared to England and Wales. However, Scotland saw a considerable decline of these 'other' communal medical and care establishments for older residents from 1991 to 2001.

Conclusions

It will interesting to see if in the next decade the number of care homes in Scotland plateaus, as it seems to have done in other regions of the country before going into slight decline. For example, the Edinburgh Community Care Plan for 2002–05 talks of trying to locate older people leaving long-term hospital beds directly in the community rather than in smaller communal establishments like nursing homes and rest homes. There have been important policy differences after 2001. The Scottish Executive responded very positively to Stewart Sutherland's (1999) Royal Commission on Long Term Care, moving quickly to encourage more generous levels of public support and subsidy, but this does not explain the different trend in care home development that happened from 1991 to 2001.

Wales has some of the highest local area rates of self-reported limiting long-term illness in Great Britain. These high levels are possibly related to traditional working-class industries in the South, especially coal mining. However, the percentage of the population living in care homes in these areas is smaller than one might expect and there appear to be high levels of family care according to census definitions of caring. South Wales is a good example of the fact that volumes of care home provision are not always associated with areas that appear to have high levels of need for social care services.

Local authority area variations

There is likely to be continuing debate about the importance of an equitable distribution of care homes by local authority area, given the feature of exporting residents, as identified in this report. Some level of exporting is inevitable in large urban areas, given that the boundaries between metropolitan local authorities may be artificial and not based on community and kinship. Nevertheless, large amounts of inequity in the distribution of care homes between urban local authority areas may be of concern. For example, it might have an impact on ethnic minorities. People might feel under pressure to be moved away from their community, when this is not their or their families' primary choice.

There is no single factor that influences the care home market, but it is clear that market development is geographically unequal and, in some places, resistant to local government planning and intervention. There is no hard evidence that care home businesses develop in specific and local geographical places where there is an identified local authority need for their provision. This happens in some areas, but not in others. In conclusion, the idea of a market being able to respond and adapt easily to planning based on local social needs, as suggested at the time of the 1990 Act, needs further examination and understanding.

Changes in communal provision for adult social care 1991–2001

As the use of care homes evolves, and if community care expenditure continues to grow, it might be that care homes become more integrated with community care – for example, offering more short-term intensive support, such as respite care or intermediate care involving short periods of nursing home care to support hospital discharge. This might make it difficult, in local areas that have experienced a large decline in homes, to integrate residential provision effectively with local community provision. It is likely that social care will continue to have strong local aspects that reflect the needs and diversities of local communities.

Market forces will not always be responsive to the need for care homes in urban areas with high property prices. Conversely, this might play some small part in encouraging a more rapid move to home care in these areas (Robinson and Banks, 2005, p. 45). But substitution of care homes by home care is also likely to be determined by other factors, such as the nature of the local social care workforce and the motivation and commitment of local councillors and managers to the rapid development of home care services. There is no universal evidence that authorities with high rates of exporting residential care to other places and independent providers are any better at promoting the rapid development of home care services. Net exporters have higher average house prices and, in 2001, still had higher percentages of their local care home stock provided directly by local government. This illustrates the difficulty with promoting market-based care home provision in these expensive property areas. Also, urban local authorities that have the highest expenditures for supporting people in residential care tend to have the highest expenditures for supporting people in their own homes.

Possible concerns for local communities in Inner London

Inner London has proportionately less older people living in its population than most other regions in Britain. It seems likely that wealthy people choose to move out during retirement. Some stay and move only when they become frail, then being 'exported' to residential care outside Inner London, and perhaps nearer other family and friends. The King's Fund has reported that, because of high property values in London, older people who own their home and need to move into a care home find that they have to support themselves through the sale of their property and they tend to select out-of-area care homes that have private rates cheaper than London (Robinson and Banks, 2005, p. 21). This leaves the few care homes that remain in London with high proportions of publicly supported residents. Our research raises concerns that poorer older people living in social housing might also be exported away from their home community somewhat against their will when they find they are in need of care home accommodation. But our quantitative research tells us nothing about whether there is any 'choice' for the user in this process, or whether they are coerced into moving away. Recent statistics confirm that the exporting factor identified in this research is a key factor in London (Virdee and Williams, 2003). Further qualitative research is urgently needed to understand what effect exporting has on the lives of those affected.

Older people and ethnic minorities

There are similar concerns for those growing old in minority ethnic communities. Our quantitative, longitudinal data shows that the proportion of the minority ethnic population living in care homes is smaller than the rest of the population, and this was consistent from 1991 to 2001. This may be a positive finding, implying that minority ethnic communities are closer knit and better at supporting their elders, as there seems to be a particularly high level of self-reported care activity in the Asian population. However, it might also be the situation that minority ethnic populations in urban areas do not wish to be exported away from their communities into care homes that do not provide culturally sensitive services. In this situation, moving to a care home might be seen as a very negative choice. This could be a disincentive for minority ethnic older people to approach social care services for help. More qualitative research is needed to explore this situation (Mold *et al.*, 2005).

Women and care homes

Women are over-represented in care homes, even allowing for the fact that the trend is for women to outlive men and then be left without their marital partners. Women are more likely than men in their lifetime to be admitted into a care home. A large majority of all care home residents (63 per cent in 2001) are women aged 75 and over.

Much has been written about the burden of social care activity in society falling on women and women who may be isolated carers at home (Ungerson, 1998). It is ironic that women are over-represented in institutional care at a time when they need to receive home-based care themselves to allow them to retain their independence and dignity for as long as possible. Older women whose previous marital partner has died may be quite isolated within the care home environment, and lacking in regular visits and contacts from outside the institution. This may reduce the quality of care experienced. There needs to be qualitative research to examine the extent to which women make choices or not about their transition into residential care.

Changes in communal provision for adult social care 1991–2001

Age groups

Between 1991 and 2001 there were some noticeable changes in the age structure of the care home population. A large majority of care homes residents were still older people, but the average age had increased and there was in 2001 a larger number of those 85 and over when compared to 1991, even though the total care home population had declined. A key feature in 2001 was also the rising number of those aged 95 and over.

Younger adults

The population of care homes is predominantly 65 and over (86 per cent of the care home population in 2001), but there are some particular features of care home residents between the ages of 16 and 64. This 'younger' care home population is predominantly male. Between 1991 and 2001 the average age of this younger care home population increased. The only 'younger' age grouping that declined in its proportion of the total care home population was the 16–29 age group (declining from 3 per cent to 2.5 per cent).

Census figures do not demonstrate a dramatic decline in the numbers of people aged 16–64 living in care homes, because of higher numbers in the 30 and over age groups. This may be because of a policy of 'gradual transition' from institutions to the community, with care homes being used as transitions from the older and larger institutions such as psychiatric hospitals. Further research is needed to see if there should have been more quantitative movement of peoples into care facilities where residents have much more independence.

Coastal and rural areas

The lowest ratios of supported residents to all people living in care homes in the local area were found in coastal areas in the South East and South West of England. Therefore it seems likely that these areas also have large numbers of residents who have been exported from other areas, in particular urban areas. In other words, non-coastal areas are paying for a proportion of the supported fees in these coastal areas. Coastal areas must also have large numbers of private fee payers who are not supported by any local government involvement. These coastal local areas had the highest average proportions of older residents living in care homes. Rural areas have similar percentages of older residents living in care homes, with only a marginally lower average figure than coastal areas. Nevertheless, the coastal areas still tended to suffer overall decline in the number of homes between 1991 and 2001. Previous researchers have written of the complex policy difficulties for one area in the South West of England when its generous levels of care home provision began to decline (Andrews and Phillips, 2002).

Poverty and residential care

The data suggested that poorer sections of the population were likely to have been under-represented in care homes, with the tendency that, the more deprived a local authority area, the greater the decline in the number of care homes. Areas with a larger proportion of older people in households with a limiting long-term illness and 'not of good health' are more likely to be socially deprived and to have lower proportions of older people living in care homes. Exporting residents complicates this picture, however, and it may be that poorer residents in urban areas are more likely to be provided with care in an area other than their own. There are concerns, as with other public services, that care homes are not necessarily located where they are most socially needed.

Working with the market to meet local social needs

The 1990 NHS and Community Care Act was an important attempt to end the dominance of residential care as the primary form of social care provision. Much was written by academics and policy analysts during the 1990s about the need for local and central government to manage and plan the newly emerging, diverse social care market, so as to ensure that it met social need on an equitable basis. It is difficult to conclude that central and local government were very successful at needs-based planning, perhaps because, in the main, market forces were rather out of government control. But the care home sector has continued to play a very central role in the delivery and experience of social care for many people.

Care home provision tends to be more abundant in areas with the largest proportions of people aged 75 and over, but these areas are not necessarily the local places with the highest levels of limiting long-term illness among the older population, and so these areas do not necessarily have the greatest need for care services.

Changes in communal provision for adult social care 1991–2001

In the current policy environment, which seeks to encourage the more rapid development of personal and home care services, it is important to recognise the part that care homes will continue to play in any future social and health care policy developments and changes. This is increasingly likely to be negotiated between local health organisations and local government, which will need to be especially careful about any decommissioning decisions in respect to adult residential care.

Notes

Chapter 1

1 Laing and Buisson, http://www.laingbuisson.co.uk/.

2 For further details, see Appendix 2.

3 There were a few areas (mostly in Scotland) where complex boundary changes complicated this process. See Appendix 2 for further details.

Chapter 2

1 For discussion of the different trends evident in Scotland and England and Wales, see the conclusion.

2 The reliability of the census distinction between residential and nursing homes was felt to be questionable. Reasons for this included the lack of a category for dual-registered homes on the census form and issues around the exclusion of very small care homes.

3 As noted in the introduction, the decline in residents may be somewhat inflated because of an undercount in the 2001 resident figures.

Chapter 3

1 Department of Health (2001) Table S2, derived from form SR1 (available at www.doh.gov.uk).

2 It should be noted, though, that this may not be the case where the difference is marginal because of some undercount in care home resident statistics in the 2001 Census.

3 'Urban' areas included all metropolitan boroughs and unitary authorities in England, plus Cardiff, Swansea, Edinburgh, Glasgow, Aberdeen and Dundee. All other local authority areas of Great Britain were classified as 'rural/mixed'.

4   Classification derived from Vickers *et al.* (2003). (See Appendix 2 for further details.)

5   Classification derived from Vickers *et al.* (2003). (See Appendix 2 for further details.)

6   Independent *t* test result: urban: (M = 8.7, SD = 81.9); rural/mixed: (M = –12.2, SD = 39.2) $t(106)$ = 2.14, p = 0.034.

7   Classification derived from Vickers *et al.* (2003). (See Appendix 2 for further details.)

8   Classification derived from Vickers *et al.* (2003). (See Appendix 2 for further details.)

9   Urban: p <0.0005, r = –0.358; rural/mixed: p = 0.352, r = –0.165.

10 Scotland: p = 0.722, r = –0.066; Wales: p = 0.203, r = 0.283.

11 Scotland: p = 0.953, r = –0.011; Wales: p = 0.460, r = –0.166.

12 However, it has been suggested that cultural factors may have affected the likelihood of a positive answer to the question on LLTI. This may have been influential in the Welsh and Scottish differences in Senior (1998).

13 Independent *t* test result: urban: (M = 19.2, SD = 2.6); rural/mixed: (M = 17.0, SD = 2.4) $t(214)$ = 7.8, p <0.0005.

Chapter 4

1   Data derived from Tables LBS04, SAS02, ST001 and ST126 (the same results are also found using the SAR).

2   The apparent over-representation of younger men in care homes may be related to the higher incidence of learning disabilities among males than females (average ratio 1.2 males: 1 female). See 'Statistics on learning disabilities' at: http://www.learningdisabilities.org.uk/page.cfm?pagecode=ISBISTBI (accessed 24 November 2005).

Notes

Chapter 5

1. It should also be noted that cases for which ethnicity was imputed were excluded in this analysis since the authors were advised of concerns over the accuracy of imputed ethnic groups.

2. Including those of an Indian, Pakistani or Bangladeshi origin (but not Chinese).

3. Including black/black British and Chinese and other.

4. And 43 per cent of the 75+ population.

5. Comparative data was not available for 1991.

6. There is, for example, no data on carers by ethnicity.

7. For a discussion on the problems with this variable see Chapter 6.

8. Outer London: $p<0.0005$; Inner London: $p=0.857$.

9. Pakistani and Indian populations combined comprise 4.7 per cent of the Inner London and 10.3 per cent of the Outer London population. No other minority ethnic group comprised a larger proportion of the Outer London than Inner London populations except Asian or Asian British other (which does not include Bangladeshi or Chinese).

10. For Asian (including Asian/Asian British: Indian, Pakistani, Bangladeshi and other as well as Chinese) $p<0.0005$, $r=0.810$; for black (including black/black British: Caribbean, African, other) $p=0.042$, $r=0.470$).

11. $p=0.882$.

12. Scotland was not included in this analysis, as the ethnic group categories were not consistent with the England and Wales categories.

13. This is also evident in the 1991 SAR, in which 34 per cent of the older Asian (75+) group live in households with six or more persons.

Changes in communal provision for adult social care 1991-2001

Chapter 6

1 In England, total households receiving home care declined by 20 per cent between 1992 and 1999 (General Household Survey, 1999, ONS). In Scotland, total clients receiving home care declined by 30 per cent between 1995 and 2001 (SEHD Community Care Statistics, 2001). However expenditure rose because of the increase in intensive home care.

2 The 2001 Census question on unpaid care reads: 'Do you look after or give any support or help to family members, friends, neighbours or others because of a) a long-term limiting illness or disability or b) problems relating to old age?' The 1991 Census form did not include a question about unpaid care.

3 Men aged 75+ providing unpaid care: Scotland = 8.4 per cent, England = 11.4 per cent, Wales = 12.5 per cent. Women aged 75+ providing care: Scotland = 4.7 per cent, England = 6.2 per cent, Wales = 6.4 per cent.

4 Data on households with two or more persons with an LLTI that have a carer living in the household (which could be one of the persons with an LLTI) is also available but is not broken down into age groups.

5 Overall numbers of over 75s living alone increased in this period but, as a percentage of all persons over 75, there was a slight decline.

Appendix 1

1 Health and Personal Social Services for Northern Ireland.

2 Census data shows that, for Northern Ireland as a whole, there was little change in the number of NHS/HSSB homes and hospitals, from 136 in 1991 to 135 in 2001. Department of Health, Social Services and Public Safety (DHSSPS) data, however, shows that statutory residential care home places declined by 42 per cent between 1991 and 2001, while the private/voluntary sector increased by 9 per cent (however, this increase is inflated because 2001 private home data includes dual-registered homes).

Appendix 2

1 Counties/metropolitan areas that are not listed were not affected by boundary changes.

2 1991 area renamed.

3 This is a rough approximation, as Boothferry was divided in two between East Riding of Yorkshire and North Lincolnshire.

4 The reorganisation of Scotland was more complex than detailed in this Appendix, as some districts and even wards in Strathclyde and Tayside were divided between various new local authority areas. However, for the purposes of this research, where the majority of a district formed a new local authority area, then the whole of the district was allocated as such.

References

Andrews, G.J. and Phillips, D.R (2002) 'Changing local geographies of private residential care for older people 1983-1999: lessons for social policy in England and Wales', *Social Science and Medicine*, Vol. 55, No. 1, pp. 63–78

Audit Commission (1986) *Making a Reality of Community Care*. London: HMSO.

Bulmer, M. (1987) *The Social Basis of Community Care*. London: Macmillan

Coms-Herrera, A., Wittenberg, R. and Pickard, L. (2001) *Projections of Demand for Residential Care for Older People in England to 2020*. PSSRU Discussion Paper 1719. Canterbury: University of Kent at Canterbury

Dale, A. and Marsh, C. (eds) (1993) *The 1991 Census User's Guide*. London: HMSO

Department of Health (1989) *Caring for People. Community Care in the Next Decade and Beyond*. London: HMSO

Department of Health (2001) *Community Care Statistics 2001: Residential Personal Social Services for Adults, England*. Ref. 2001/0577. London: Department of Health. www.doh.gov.uk

Department of Health (2002) *Personal Social Services Expenditure and Unit Costs, England, 2000–2001*. London: Department of Health

Department of Health (2004) *Health and Social Care Statistics*. London: Department of Health. http://www.performance.doh.gov.uk/

Department of Health (2005) *Independence, Well-being and Choice: Our Vision for the Future of Social Care for Adults in England*. Green Paper. London: Department of Health. http://www.doh.gov.uk/

Griffiths, R. (1989) *Community Care: Agenda for Action. A Report to the Secretary of State for Social Services*. London: HMSO

Grundy, E. and Glaser, K. (1997) 'Trends in, and transitions to, institutional residence among older people in England and Wales, 1971–1991', *Journal of Epidemiology and Community Health*, Vol. 51, pp. 531–40

References

House of Commons Health Committee (1996) *Long-term Care: Future Provision and Funding. Volume 1.* London: The Stationery Office

Knapp, M., Hardy, B. and Forder, J. (2001) 'Commissioning for quality: ten years of social care markets in England', *Journal of Social Policy*, Vol. 30, pp. 283–306

Mold, F., Fitzpatrick, J.M. and Roberts, J.D. (2005) 'Minority ethnic elders in care homes: a review of the literature', *Age and Ageing*, Vol. 34, No. 2, pp. 107–13

National Audit Office (NAO) (2003) *Ensuring the Effective Discharge of Older Patients from NHS Acute Hospitals.* London: NAO

Office for National Statistics, General Register Office for Scotland and Northern Ireland Statistics and Research Agency (2004) *Census 2001: Definitions.* London: The Stationery Office

Office of Fair Trading (OFT) (2005) *Care Homes for Older People in the UK: A Market Study.* London: OFT

Rallings, C. and Thrasher M. (1999) *British Parliamentary Election Results 1983–1998.* Aldershot: Ashgate

Robinson, J. and Banks, P. (2005) *The Business of Caring: King's Fund Inquiry into Care Services for Older People in London.* London: King's Fund

Senior, M. (1998) 'Area variations in self-perceived limiting long-term illness in Britain, 1991. Is the Welsh experience exceptional?', *Regional Studies*, Vol. 32, May, pp. 265–80

Sutherland, S. (1999) *With Respect to Old Age: Long Term Care – Rights and Responsibilities. A Report by The Royal Commission on Long Term Care.* Cm. 4192-I. London: The Stationery Office

Ungerson, C. (ed.) (1998) *Women and Social Policy: A Reader.* Basingstoke: Macmillan

Vickers, D., Rees, P. and Birkin, M. (2003) *A New Classification of UK Local Authorities Using 2001 Census Key Statistics.* Leeds: University of Leeds

Virdee, D. and Williams, T. (eds) (2003) *Focus on London 2003.* Report for the National Statistics Office, London Development Agency, Greater London Authority and Government Office for London. London: The Stationery Office

Appendix 1: Northern Ireland

Comparison of 1991 and 2001 data

Northern Ireland census data on care homes for 2001 is not fully comparable with 1991. Only the independent sector data is comparable, since, in the 1991 Census, statutory homes are included under the category: 'NHS hospitals and homes'. No comparison can therefore be made with the 2001 data on NHS/Health and Social Services Boards (HSSB)[1] nursing and residential care home establishments.[2] The data provided in Table A1.1 therefore includes only independent sector homes (nursing and residential) and residents for 1991 and 2001. This shows that, although several areas experienced a significant decline, there was a slight overall increase in independent sector homes (1 per cent) and residents (6 per cent).

Table A1.1 Independent sector homes and residents 1991–2001 by Northern Ireland council area

Council area	Homes 1991	Homes 2001	Change homes No.	Change homes %	Residents 1991	Residents 2001	Change residents No.	Change residents %
Antrim	14	13	−1	−7	313	175	−138	−44
Ards	20	21	1	5	429	420	−9	−2
Armagh	15	16	1	7	383	440	57	15
Ballymena	13	14	1	8	225	364	139	62
Ballymoney	7	8	1	14	119	82	−37	−31
Banbridge	5	8	3	60	56	153	97	173
Belfast	107	74	−33	−31	2,227	1,797	−430	−19
Carrickfergus	9	9	0	0	200	169	−31	−16
Castlereagh	9	15	6	67	294	408	114	39
Coleraine	12	19	7	58	417	505	88	21
Cookstown	6	6	0	0	167	172	5	3
Craigavon	14	12	−2	−14	320	389	69	22
Derry	13	22	9	69	293	490	197	67
Down	37	26	−11	−30	656	592	−64	−10
Dungannon	9	11	2	22	224	252	28	13
Fermanagh	10	21	11	110	234	410	176	75
Larne	9	9	0	0	171	119	−52	−30
Limavady	3	6	3	100	92	109	17	18
Lisburn	19	21	2	11	385	552	167	43
Magherafelt	6	10	4	67	100	98	−2	−2
Moyle	8	7	−1	−13	198	96	−102	−52
Newry and Mourne	25	14	−11	−44	602	349	−253	−42

(Continued)

Appendix 1

Table A1.1 Independent sector homes and residents 1991–2001 by Northern Ireland council area (Continued)

Council area	Homes 1991	Homes 2001	Change homes No.	Change homes %	Residents 1991	Residents 2001	Change residents No.	Change residents %
Newtownabbey	18	16	−2	−11	423	492	69	16
North Down	28	31	3	11	491	833	342	70
Omagh	7	17	10	143	186	228	42	23
Strabane	3	4	1	33	64	131	67	105
Northern Ireland	426	432	6	1	9,269	9,825	556	6

Sources: Census Tables SAS03, UV72, ST301.

2001 data

Proportion living in care homes by age group

As shown in Table A1.2, there were some areas of Northern Ireland where a low proportion of over 75's were living in care homes (notably, Magherafelt: 2 per cent). However, in comparison with the other countries of the UK, there was a high proportion of over 75's living in care homes in 2001 (8.3 per cent). In fact, the proportion of people in both the 75–84 (4.8 per cent) and the 85 or over (19.7 per cent) age group who were living in residential or nursing homes was higher in Northern Ireland than in any other region of the UK. The proportion of people in the younger age group (16–74) was also relatively high (0.25 per cent), but slightly lower than in the South West and South East of England (see Tables 3 and 19, and Figure 13 to compare the Northern Ireland data with data for other areas of the UK).

Figure A1.1 shows how the 2001 age distribution in care homes in Northern Ireland differed from the rest of the UK, with a higher proportion of people in the younger age groups and a smaller proportion over 80. This to some extent reflects the age profile of Northern Ireland as a whole, which is younger than in England and Scotland and Wales (as can be seen in Figure 16). In fact, Northern Ireland in 2001 had a similar age profile to London, with only 5.9 per cent of people aged 75+ in both regions. Since, in the other parts of the UK, there is a positive association between the proportion of older people in a region and the proportion living in care homes (see Figure 18), the relatively high proportion living in care homes in Northern Ireland is untypical.

Changes in communal provision for adult social care 1991–2001

Table A1.2 Percentage of people aged 75 and over who live in care homes, 2001

Council area	%
Antrim	6.9
Ards	8.7
Armagh	9.9
Ballymena	8.4
Ballymoney	4.6
Banbridge	8.2
Belfast	7.9
Carrickfergus	7.7
Castlereagh	8.1
Coleraine	10.1
Cookstown	9.6
Craigavon	7.0
Down	13.5
Dungannon	8.1
Fermanagh	8.1
Larne	6.3
Limavady	6.5
Lisburn	9.1
Londonerry/Derry	9.0
Magherafelt	2.2
Moyle	10.0
Newry and Mourne	5.0
Newtonabbey	9.1
North Down	10.9
Omagh	5.7
Strabane	6.5
Northern Ireland	8.3

Sources: Census Tables KS02, ST301.

Appendix 1

Figure A1.1 Age distribution in care homes in Northern Ireland and Great Britain, 2001

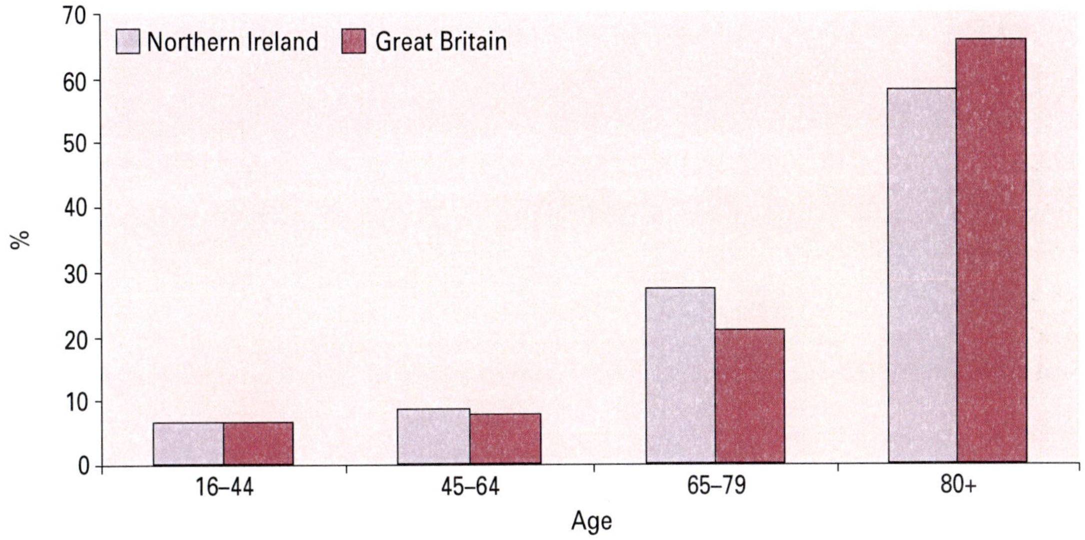

Source: 2001 Sample of Anonymised Records.

Gender and marital status

Table A1.3 shows the proportion of men/women in each age group by gender, for both the care home and the total population in 2001. Comparative data for other regions of the UK is provided in Table 12. The two tables present a similar pattern in terms of the under-representation of men in the older age groups and the over-representation of men in the younger age groups. The difference is, however, more prominent in Northern Ireland, as, although there was a larger proportion of men in the 80+ total population (35 per cent compared with 32 per cent in GB), a smaller proportion of people in the 80+ age group in care homes were male (13 per cent compared with 18 per cent in GB). Also, there was a larger proportion of men in care homes in the 45–64 group in Northern Ireland (61 per cent compared with 56 per cent in GB), even though the proportion in the total population was about the same (50 per cent).

Table A1.3 Percentage in each age group of the care home population and the total population by gender in Northern Ireland, 2001

Age group	Men Care homes	Men Total population	Women Care homes	Women Total population
16–44	59.1	49.5	40.9	50.5
45–64	60.7	50.0	39.3	50.0
65–79	33.7	44.5	66.3	55.5
80 and over	13.6	34.8	86.4	65.2

Source: 2001 Sample of Anonymised Records.

Changes in communal provision for adult social care 1991–2001

The relatively small proportion of older men living in care homes is also highlighted in Table A1.4, which allows comparison of the proportion living in care homes for each age, gender and marital status group in Northern Ireland with those for Great Britain. It shows that, of all the gender/age groups, only men aged 85+ (both married and unmarried) were better represented in care homes in Great Britain than in Northern Ireland. In particular, older married women in Northern Ireland were much more likely to be living in a care home than their counterparts in Great Britain. Nevertheless, married persons in all age/gender groups were less likely to live in a care home than those who were not married.

Table A1.4 Percentage in each age group of the care home population in Northern Ireland and Great Britain by gender and marital status, 2001

Age group	Men Married NI	GB	Unmarried NI	GB	Women Married NI	GB	Unmarried NI	GB	Total Married NI	GB	Unmarried NI	GB
16–74	0.1	0.1	0.6	0.5	0.1	0.1	0.5	0.4	0.1	0.1	0.5	0.4
75–84	1.6	1.1	7.4	5.6	4.1	1.5	8.4	5.8	2.6	1.3	8.2	5.8
85 and over	5.4	5.9	10.6	17.0	19.5	9.3	24.7	22.4	9.7	7.1	22.0	21.4

Source: 2001 Sample of Anonymised Records.
Note: 'Married' combines categories: 'married', 'remarried' and 'separated'; 'unmarried' combines categories: 'single', 'widowed' and 'divorced'.

Household structure and other forms of care

The 2001 data for Northern Ireland particularly stands out against the hypothesis that there would be a higher proportion of people receiving unpaid care in areas with lower rates of residential care. In addition to having the highest proportion of older people in residential care of any UK region, Northern Ireland also had the largest proportion of people reporting to provide any unpaid care (11.0 per cent) and 20+ hours unpaid care (4.5 per cent), except for Wales (with 11.7 per cent/4.6 per cent respectively). This is particularly noteworthy when the much younger profile of the population in Northern Ireland is taken into account.

In Northern Ireland, in 2001, the proportion of older people living in lone-person households was smaller, and conversely the proportion living in two+-person households greater, than any other region of the UK. There was also a relatively high proportion living in other medical care establishments (at 0.6 per cent) – lower only than London at 0.7 per cent. The proportions of older people living in the various types of household/establishments in Northern Ireland can be compared with those for Great Britain in Table A1.5 (for a full comparison of the regions see Table 19).

Appendix 1

Table A1.5 Living arrangements of people aged 75 and over by region, 2001 (per cent)

Region	Care homes	Other medical/ care establishments	In household – alone	In household – 2+/other*
Northern Ireland	8.3	0.6	40.5	50.7
Great Britain	6.6	0.4	43.8	49.1

Sources: KS02, ST301, T46.
* 'Other' refers to the small number living in non-medical/care establishments.

The reasons for the apparent higher rates of residential and unpaid care in Northern Ireland than other areas of the UK are unclear and would require further research. However, the relatively high rates of limiting-long term illness (as apparent in Figure 21) in Northern Ireland should be noted. In the 75+ age bracket, 68.2 per cent of people in Northern Ireland reported to have a limiting-long term illness, which was higher than any other region and compares with 62.7 for Great Britain.

Appendix 2: Geographical areas 1991/2001

Table A2.1 details how 1991 district areas for each county/regional council correspond to the county/unitary authority areas applicable to the 2001 Census.[1]

Table A2.1 Geographical areas 1991/2001

1991 district(s)	2001 local authority area
England	
Avon	
Northavon and Kingswood	South Gloucestershire[2] (UA)
Woodspring	North Somerset[2] (UA)
Wansdyke and Bath	Bath and North East Somerset[2] (UA)
Bristol	Bristol (UA)
Bedford	
North Bedford + Mid Bedfordshire + South Bedfordshire	Bedfordshire
Luton	Luton (UA)
Berkshire	
Reading	Reading (UA)
Wokingham	Wokingham (UA)
Windsor and Maidenhead	Windsor and Maidenhead (UA)
Slough	Slough (UA)
Bracknell Forest	Bracknell Forest (UA)
Newbury	West Berkshire[2] (UA)
Buckinghamshire	
Aylesbury Vale + Wycombe + Chiltern and South Buckinghamshire	Buckinghamshire
Milton Keynes	Milton Keynes (UA)
Cambridgeshire	
Fenland + Huntingdonshire + East Cambridgeshire + South Cambridgeshire + Cambridge	Cambridgeshire
Peterborough	Peterborough (UA)
Cheshire	
Ellesmere Port and Neston + Chester + Vale Royal + Macclesfield + Crewe and Nantwich + Congleton	Cheshire
Halton	Halton (UA)
Warrington	Warrington (UA)
Cleveland	
Hartlepool	Hartlepool (UA)
Stockton-on-Tees	Stockton-on-Tees (UA)
Middlesbrough	Middlesbrough (UA)
Langbaurgh-on-Tees	Redcar and Cleveland[2] (UA)

(Continued)

Appendix 2

Table A2.1 Geographical areas 1991/2001 (Continued)

1991 district(s)	2001 local authority area
Derbyshire	
High Peak + Derbyshire Dales + North East Derbyshire + Chesterfield + Bolsover + Amber Valley + Erewash + South Derbyshire	Derbyshire
Derby	Derby (UA)
Devon	
Torridge + North Devon + West Devon + Mid Devon + Teignbridge + Exeter + East Devon + South Hams	Devon
Plymouth	Plymouth (UA)
Torbay	Torbay (UA)
Dorset	
West Dorset + North Dorset + East Dorset + Weymouth + Portland + Purbeck + Christchurch	Dorset
Poole	Poole (UA)
Bournemouth	Bournemouth (UA)
Durham	
Wear Valley + Derwentside + Chester-Le-Street + Durham + Easlington + Teesdale + Sedgefield	Durham
Darlington	Darlington (UA)
East Sussex	
Lewes + Rother + Wealden + Hastings + Eastbourne	East Sussex
Brighton + Hove	Brighton and Hove (UA)
Essex	
Uttlesford + Braintree + Colchester + Tendring + Harlow + Epping Forest + Chelmsford + Maldon + Brentwood + Basildon + Rochford + Castle Point	Essex
Thurrock	Thurrock (UA)
Southend-on-Sea	Southend-on-Sea (UA)
Hampshire	
Test Valley + Basingstoke + Forest of Deane + Hart + Rushmoor + Winchester + East Hampshire + New Forest + Eastleigh + Fareham + Havant + Gosport	Hampshire
Southampton	Southampton (UA)
Portsmouth	Portsmouth (UA)
Hereford and Worcester	
Leominster + South Herefordshire + Hereford	Hereford
Wyre Forest + Bromsgrove + Redditch + Malvern Hills + Worcester + Wychavon	Worcester
Humberside	
East Yorkshire + Beverley + Holderness + 50 per cent[3] of Boothferry	East Riding of Yorkshire
50 per cent[3] of Boothferry + Glanford + Scunthorpe	North Lincolnshire
Cleethorpes + Great Grimsby	North East Lincolnshire
Kingston upon Hull	Kingston upon Hull (UA)

(Continued)

Changes in communal provision for adult social care 1991–2001

Table A2.1 Geographical areas 1991/2001 (Continued)

1991 district(s)	2001 local authority area
Kent	
Dartford + Gravesham + Swale + Canterbury + Thanet + Sevenoaks + Tunbridge + Malling + Maidstone + Ashford + Shepway + Dover + Tunbridge Wells	Kent
Rochester-upon-Medway + Gillingham	Medway Towns (UA)
Lancashire	
Lancaster + Wyre + Ribble Valley + Pendle + Hynburn + Burnley + West Lancashire + South Ribble + Chorley + Rossendale	Lancashire
Blackpool	Blackpool (UA)
Blackburn	Blackburn with Darwen[2] (UA)
Leicestershire	
North West Leicestershire + Charnwood + Melton + Hinckley and Bosworth + Oadby and Wigston + Blaby + Harborough	Leicestershire
Leicester	Leicester (UA)
Rutland	Rutland (UA)
North Yorkshire	
Richmondshire + Hambleton + Ryedale + Scarborough + Craven + Harrogate + Selby	North Yorkshire
York	York (UA)
Nottinghamshire	
Bassetlow + Mansfield + Newark and Sherwood + Ashfield + Gedling + Broxtoe + Rushcliffe	Nottinghamshire
Nottingham	Nottingham (UA)
Shropshire	
Oswestry + North Shropshire + Shrewsbury and Atcham + South Shropshire + Bridgnorth	Shropshire
The Wrekin	Telford and the Wrekin (UA)
Staffordshire	
Newcastle-under-Lyme + Staffordshire Moorlands + Stafford + East Staffordshire + South Staffordshire + Cannock Chase + Lichfield + Tamworth	Staffordshire
Stoke-on-Trent	Stoke-on-Trent (UA)
Wiltshire	
North Wiltshire + West Wiltshire + Kennet + Salisbury	Wiltshire
Thamesdown	Swindon[2]
Wales	
Clywd	
Rhuddian + Glyndwr	Denbighshire
Delyn + Alyn and Deeside	Flintshire
Wrexham Maelor	Wrexham
Colwyn + Aberconwy (from Gwynedd)	Conwy

(Continued)

Appendix 2

Table A2.1 Geographical areas 1991/2001 (Continued)

1991 district(s)	2001 local authority area
Dyfed	
Preseli Pembrokeshire + South Pembrokeshire	Pembrokeshire
Ceredigion	Ceredigion
Carmarthen + Dinefwr + Llanelli	Carmarthenshire
Gwent	
Blaneau Gwent	Blaneau Gwent
Monmouthshire[2]	Monmouth
Torfaen	Torfaen
Newport	Newport
Isylwyn + Rhymney Valley (from Mid Glamorgan)	Caerphilly
Gwynedd	
Arfon + Dwyfor + Meirionnydd	Gwynedd
Aberconwy joins with Colwyn (Conwy)	
Mid Glamorgan	
Ogwr (Bridgend)	Ogwr
Rhondda + Cynon Valley + Taff-Ely	Rhondda Cynon Taff
Merthyr Tydfil	Merthyr Tydfil
Rhymney Valley joins with Isylwyn (Caerphilly)	
South Glamorgan	
Vale of Glamorgan	Vale of Glamorgan
Cardiff	Cardiff
West Glamorgan	
Swansea + Lilw Valley	Swansea
Neath + Port Talbot	Neath & Port Talbot
Scotland[4]	
Borders	Scottish Borders
Central	
Clackmannan	Clackmannanshire
Falkirk	Falkirk
Stirling	Stirling
Dumfries and Galloway	Dumfries and Galloway
Fife	Fife
Grampian	
Aberdeen City	Aberdeen City
Banff and Buchan + Gordon + Kincardine and Deeside	Aberdeenshire
Moray	Moray
Highland	Highland
Lothian	
East Lothian	East Lothian
Edinburgh City	Edinburgh City
Midlothian	Midlothian
West Lothian	West Lothian

(Continued)

Changes in communal provision for adult social care 1991–2001

Table A2.1 Geographical areas 1991/2001 (Continued)

1991 district(s)	2001 local authority area
Strathclyde	
Argyll and Bute	Argyll and Bute
Bearsden and Milngavie + Strathkelvin	East Dunbartonshire
Clydebank + Dumbarton	West Dunbartonshire
Cumbernauld and Kilsyth + Monklands + Motherwell	North Lanarkshire
Cumnock and Doon Valley + Kilmarnock and Loudon	East Ayrshire
Cunninghame	North Ayrshire
East Kilbride + Clydesdale + Hamilton	South Lanarkshire
Eastwood	East Renfrewshire
Glasgow City	Glasgow City
Inverclyde	Inverclyde
Kyle and Carrick	South Ayrshire
Renfrew	Renfrewshire
Tayside	
Angus	Angus
Dundee City	Dundee City
Perth and Kinross	Perth and Kinross
Orkney	Orkney Islands
Shetland	Shetland Islands
Western Isles	Eilean Siar (Western Isles)

Appendix 3: Census information

The main outputs from the 1991 and 2001 Censuses are a large number of standard tables that cross-tabulate a selection of variables. An individual database is not available for the entire Census and all its variables. This is because of national legislation that protects confidentiality and anonymity. There is, however, a sample of the national database called the Sample of Anonymised Records (SARs), which offers researchers greater aspects of flexibility to choose what variables are analysed.

This research project used data taken from the standard tables for the purpose of looking at the overall national trend change in the availability of residential social care establishments and number of residents between 1991 and 2001. This analysis is carried out at the local authority and regional/country level.

Sample of Anonymised Records

The SARs are used for examining multivariate questions as applied to individual respondents, such as the relationship of establishment type with other variables such as age, gender, marital status and race. In other words, it is possible to examine the combined effect of age, gender and marital status on a person's likelihood of being in a residential care establishment.

When the SARs are used they represent a good national sample of the census population. The 1991 SAR used is a 2 per cent sample of the national Census. There are 1,058,000 people in the sample with a sub-sample of 8,513 in residential and nursing care.

The 2001 SAR used a 3 per cent sample of the national Census. There are 1,843,530 people in the sample with a sub-sample of 12,119 residents in residential and nursing care.

In most situations this sub-sample is of adequate size to present probability calculations that are significant and can be generalised to country and regional findings, but social care authority, local authority areas are too small to yield significant results and are likely to be invalid and unrepresentative. The ability to make valid inferences about individuals, when using the SARs, is limited when focusing on small sub-sample groups such as residents in care homes by local area and the minority ethnic residents in care homes at regional level.

Changes in communal provision for adult social care 1991–2001

Definitions

The 1991 Census defines 'communal' as a residence where 'some kind of communal catering is provided' (Dale and Marsh, 1993, p. 24). In 2001, the census definition of a communal establishment evolved to: 'an establishment providing managed residential accommodation. "Managed" means full time or part time supervision of the accommodation' (Office for National Statistics *et al.*, 2004, pp. 18, 24). The 2001 Census treats buildings as communal establishments only if there are ten or more residents in addition to the owner/manager and his/her family, whereas the 1991 Census treated buildings as communal establishments if they had more than ten rooms. Both the Censuses therefore exclude very small homes (these are likely to be classified as large households). Our research therefore undercounts the number of small residential care establishments. Some cross-checking with the data set of Laing and Buisson and similarly with the Department of Health statistics office confirms an element of undercounting in our data set. For example, it appears that the Department of Health in 2001 counted the number of care homes in England as about 30 per cent higher than the 2001 Census categories for residential and nursing homes, this based on local authority returns to the Department (Department of Health, 2001). Much of this difference can be attributed to the 2001 Census not counting small homes, although our research also excludes some housing association provision. Our estimate is that our undercounting of homes is likely to have a fairly equal effect in both 1991 and 2001.

There is also likely to be some further undercounting of residents in the 2001 Census, this in addition to the omission of those living in small care homes. The National Statistics Office (NSO) has recently reported a concern that some people coded as care home staff in the 2001 Census were really residents. This miscoding apparently happened because of the way in which a 2001 Census question was worded. This was discovered in the results when the NSO found a number of staff over 75 who, it seems, must have been residents. Full details of the likely effects of this unreliability were not available at the time of publishing this report. This unreliability affects the 2001 data but, as far as we know, not the 1991 data.

There were 18 major categories of communal establishment in 1991, including hospitals and other medical and social care establishments (Dale and Marsh, 1993). The key census categories of interest to this research are:

- local authority homes

- nursing homes (non NHS/local authority/health authority) *private and independent sector*

Appendix 3

- residential homes (non NHS/local authority/health authority) *private and independent sector.*

It should be noted there are also categories not included in our research. These include: housing association homes and hostels; children's homes, hostels and boarding houses; and other miscellaneous establishments. The numbers in these categories are small and were not judged to be of general relevance to this research.

In 1991, sheltered housing was classified as a communal establishment if less than half the residents had facilities for cooking their own meals. This remains consistent in the 2001 definition. Our research has not included sheltered housing in the analysis.

There were some changes in the categories of communal establishment presented in the 2001 Census. The following categories were of interest to the research:

- local authority residential homes

- local authority other homes

- other nursing homes

- other residential homes.

In addition there are categories for: housing association home or hostel, local authority children's homes, other children's homes, other medical and care home, other psychiatric hospital or home, and some categories for general hostels and boarding houses.

The main differences between the two key groups of categories used from 1991 and 2001 are the additional local authority sub-groupings for the 2001 Census. For the purposes of this research project, these groupings are computed together into one local authority homes category. The local authority sub-divisions did not seem particularly useful to the examination of cross-sectional change and related policy developments.

There is also the matter of the definition of the people living in the categories of care homes used. In 1991 these people were classified into four groups:

Changes in communal provision for adult social care 1991–2001

- resident staff

- resident relatives of staff

- resident non-staff

- visitors and guests.

Visitors were those who had still regarded themselves as having a permanent residence elsewhere, so it is possible this might have included a very small number of new residents, or temporary and short-term residents.

In 2001, the census enumerator did not have to make decisions about visitors. There were three categories of people:

- staff/owner

- relative of staff/owner

- other.

Our research excludes staff, relatives and visitors, and attempts to analyse only the number of residents.